Interview Questions

How To Build Confidence And Get Any Job You Want, With 100 Great Answers To Tough Questions That Employers Would Ask

Table of Contents

Introduction

I want to thank you and congratulate you for downloading the book, "Interview: How To Build Confidence And Get Any Job You Want, With 100 Great Answers To Tough Questions That Employers Would Ask"

Interviews can make anyone nervous. But if you simply let go of your nervousness, you'll find that you'll do much better. Keep in mind that this is hard for the interviewer too, as he or she gets to know you. To get you started, you need to practice your answers and learn how to time them. But even with all the preparation, you should avoid talking for more than two minutes nonstop and memorizing your answers verbatim. The answers revealed in this book should only be used as a guide; you can also include your own words and thoughts. For instance, you can note down and assess some key words for every answer.

To improve your interviewing skills, try to practice your answers on a regular basis, and you will find them coming naturally during your interviews. In essence, the most significant strategy, when it comes to interviews, is to identify what people are looking for, and then show them your contribution towards achieving it. Find out what your potential employers are looking for in their candidates, and then show them your qualifications. In simple terms, you need to match the needs of your potential employer with your abilities. You must possess what the employer is buying.

Think of an interview as a situation similar to going to the grocery store to purchase necessary items; the seller has to convince you to buy his or her product. In the same way, the interviewer here is the buyer; so you should convince him or her to buy your product i.e. the value you bring to the business. After all, no one would buy anything out of pity for the seller or purchase a product that does not meet his or her expectations. As such, the idea is to present the very best that you have to offer.

In order to do this, you need to find out what they are looking for in the first place, and the best approach is to ask yourself a few questions.

Learn to be more optimistic every day. For instance, try taking a positive perspective on situations and events you would otherwise consider negative. In simple words, try sharpening your selling skills. As a general rule of thumb, the more promising candidates, as well as the best salespeople, have the ability to portray natural optimism. When you learn to be more optimistic, you will drastically improve your degree of attractiveness. Be honest and never lie.

This book is aimed at helping you package your product (skills) well to persuade the buyer (interviewer). Let's get started.

Thanks again for downloading this book, I hope you enjoy it!

Getting Started

Now that you have applied for a job and impressed the prospective employer, you are one step closer to getting the job. While this is obviously good news, I know it creates some sense of anxiety and stress just because it is a new experience. You will tend to have thoughts like "what if I mess up", "what should I wear," "how am I going to go through the interview," "what do I do to maximize my chances of success?" etc. While all these are legitimate concerns, you need to gather enough courage to prepare yourself for the interview. Here are some of the things you need to understand as you prepare for the interview:

→ **For starters, you need to know the nature of the job so that you can dress appropriately. You don't want to show up when you are inappropriately dressed for the interview. Find out what people in that profession normally wear for interviews; then look for appropriate attire for that.**

→ **Learn as much as possible about the company in question. Don't just show up blindly with zero information about the company you want to work for. You need to know the ins and outs about the company because some of this information will help you to answer questions in the interview correctly and authoritatively. Besides, it helps you to boost your confidence levels greatly.**

→ **Your confidence is probably your best asset when going to an interview. Even with all the preparation, you can be sure that you will definitely come across a few questions that will catch you off guard, or you might have forgotten some of the things you learned during your preparation. Having confidence will help you in such situations because you will definitely not panic even when you don't know the answer to some interview questions. The best way to build confidence** in an interview situation is to know your stuff, i.e.: research as much as possible about the company and the industry just to make sure that you feel authoritative about any question that relates to such issues.

→ Paired with confidence, your mindset will work to your advantage. You want to have the mindset that the interviewers are not there to torment you or don't like your dress code, your height, your hairstyle or anything else about you. Having the right mindset about the interview will work a long way in making you to feel confident about yourself. For instance, you'll avoid freaking out over a spontaneous, unplanned response just because you could not answer a question properly. You can try positive self-talk so that you can develop a positive mindset.

→ Work on your anxiety: Well, you might probably fight some of the anxiety through preparation, but if you have an underlying anxiety problem, it might be too hard to "compose" yourself during an interview just because "strangers" are doing it. Use positive affirmations to help you to overcome anxiety. You can also try some relaxation exercises like deep breathing exercises or mindful meditation to help you to calm down. For more information on how to overcome anxiety please check out my other book: Anxiety self-help: http://www.amazon.com/Anxiety-self-help-Worrying-depression-ebook/dp/B017FXJ744

Part of the preparation and due diligence entails learning about the most common interview questions and how to answer them properly in order to increase your chances of being hired. In the subsequent chapters, we will cover just that.

Answers To 100 Common Interview Questions

→ **Tell me about yourself**

About 80 percent of all interviews start with this simple question. The best approach here is to begin at the present and explain why you're sufficiently qualified for the vacancy. Try to present yourself as the solution (i.e. the right candidate) for the problem at hand (i.e. the vacancy). Don't recite your resume at this time; the interviewer has it already! As you answer this question, answer the following questions:

What are your selling points for the job?

Why are you interested in this particular job now?

As you answer these, make sure you touch on:

→ **Who you are: Ensure to summarize your entire background**

→ **Your expertise: The idea is to emphasize on your experience, your enthusiasm, and your proof of performance.**

→ **Why you want the job: Be positive**

Here is a sample answer:

"I have been in the food industry for 7 years now. I was among the top chefs who elevated KFC from a local restaurant to an internationally recognized company. I most recently attended the Annual International Food Awards where I was awarded as the most innovative Chef in Europe. I am very passionate about cultural foods, and that's why I'm looking for a new challenge in your inter-cultural hotel."

→ **What are your greatest strengths?**

This may seem like a relatively simple question, but you need to be careful about coming off as arrogant or egotistical. However, you don't want to be humble at the same time. Start by uncovering the greatest needs and wants of your interviewer, and once you've answered question one correctly, you'll know how to progress from there. Here is an example:

"One of my greatest strengths is hard work. I have won 10 consecutive employee-of-the-month awards in my post as a supervisor in Jack and Jill supermarket. I'm also a good team player, something that has earned praise from our superiors for my department's performance."

> **What are your greatest weaknesses?**

Note that this question is meant to shorten the list of candidates. Admitting fault or weakness may pass you the test for honesty, but not for the interview. Let your interviewer know that there is nothing that would prevent you from giving your best in this position, and then quickly summarize your most significant qualifications. As you answer the question, ensure to address:

> **The weakness**

> **What you are doing about your weakness**

Here is a sample answer of how to answer the question:

"To be honest, I can't seem to get enough of technology. I am used to checking my phone almost every 10 minutes. Two months ago, I realized I had a problem. I am currently seeing a therapist and reading a book on how to break away from addiction. It's now three weeks into the therapy, and I have found it very effective."

> **Tell me about something you failed to do, or did, that you are ashamed of.**

This is one of those questions that's relatively none of your interviewer's business, but you naturally cannot tell them this. This question is meant to trick you into admitting to something, or see how fast you can think on your feet. Like with weaknesses and faults, never ever confess to a regret.

➤ Why did your leave (are you leaving) this position?

Never ever, badmouth your previous customers, employees, staff, boss, board, company, or industry. In short, never display negativity. Particularly, steer away from such words as "didn't get along", "personality clash", and so forth that diminish your integrity, competence, or temperament. Here is a sample on how to answer this:

"I feel like I have outgrown my position of production manager in the beverage industry. That's why I took a marketing class two years ago, and I'm now ready to take on the new challenge in your company. In addition, I have always liked marketing."

➤ The "silent treatment."

This is one of those questions that you need to be prepared for in order to handle it correctly. This strategy is used to determine how you react under stress. In case your interviewer uses it, stay silent for a while yourself, and then ask politely if there is anything else you can fill in that point. As simple as that. Here is a sample answer:

"Is there anything you would want me to fill?"

➤ Why should I hire you?

This is a very tricky question that's usually a determinant if you are not prepared for it. You need to research on the wants and needs of the employer beforehand, in order to gain an edge over other interviewees. Generally, if you give your potential employer more reason to hire you than everybody else, chances are that he will do so. Here is a sample answer:

"I am a hard working person who never backs down from a challenge. I noticed you had advertised for a position of a creative thinker in your new film production. I have 15 years of experience in this department. During my time at Dream Works Production, I ensured that their movies stood out with ideas that were out of the box. I am looking forward to offering the same level of creativity and commitment to your company."

➤ Are you not overqualified for this job?

This is usually a sign that the employer is worried that you will grow discontented and leave. Like with any opposition, do not take this as a sign of looming defeat. You can take advantage of this to present a new way of thinking, seeing benefits over disadvantages. Here is a sample answer:

"I know taking this job is a step back from the level I used to be in before, but I cannot go for a post unless I'm inspired to. The joy I got from dealing with clients was the thing that made me get into marketing in the first place. Over the years, my ranks got me further and further away from what I loved. This opportunity will reconnect me to my first love, and my 15 years of experience will really benefit you as a company."

➤ Where do you see yourself 5 years from now?

Interviewers usually use this question to find out whether you are settling into the position, or merely using it as a stop-over for something better. On the other hand, they might be gauging your sense of ambition. Reassure the employer that you are looking for a long-term commitment and that the position provides exactly what you are looking for and what you are most qualified for. Here is a sample answer:

"I would love to significantly increase the number of the client base in my next company as I perfect the art of marketing. The position in offer is perfect for my long- term goal of being the top marketer in an international company."

➤ What are your ideal job, location, and company?

This question is normally asked by experienced interviewers who think that you may be overqualified for the position. Describe what the company is offering, and use specific reasons to make your answer more believable, stating them with sincerity, and identifying why this opportunity is appealing to you through each quality.

"I have always been excited about cars even during my childhood. Being a car salesman is a dream-come-true for me; not to mention how much I wanted to work with Toyota. I feel like your company will give me an opportunity to execute my good communication skills."

➔ Why do you want to work here?

This is usually to test to see if you have done any research about the company, in which case you would lose if you haven't. Use this opportunity to set the ball rolling, taking advantage of the extensive research you assumedly did in advance. Here is a sample answer:

"According to the research I did, your company is a major player in the transport industry. I was impressed with your current project of expanding your horizons to neighboring countries, and I think my skills and experience will be of help in executing your goals."

➔ What are your career options at the moment?

This question is normally meant to test how desperate you are. Consider how you can present yourself as a wanted commodity. If you haven't left your old job yet, describe the potential at your present company and why, although you are greatly valued there, you have decided to look for something more (responsibility, money, challenge, and so forth). Here is a sample answer:

"At the moment, my career objective is to pursue a career with a reputable company, which will utilize my inter-personal skills better than my current company does."

➔ How come you've been out of work for so long?

Be careful here, as you don't want to come off as damaged goods. Emphasize the factors that have extended your job search through your own choice. Here is a sample answer:

"After our company collapsed, I decided to take some time off and sharpen my skills. I took an educational course with a goal of learning about current trends in my field of IT."

➔ Describe honestly the weak points and strong points of your boss (management team, company, etc.).

If the interviewer is very skillful, they'll make it very tempting to open up and spread some mud on your previous position. Remember, the idea is to avoid being negative. Emphasize on the good points only, regardless of how charmingly you are encouraged to be perilous. Here is a sample answer:

"My boss was very supportive. He made it his business to ask how everyone was, and he took his precious time to attend to our concerns as workers. I also had productive co-workers who brought out the best in me. The only negative thing about my boss is that he works too hard."

⇥ Tell me about some good books you have read lately

As a general rule of thumb, do not fake familiarity. However, you don't want to come off as a dullard who is completely ignorant about reading. Unless you are vying for a position in The New York Times as a book critic, they don't expect you to be a literary guru. However, reading a few influential and recent books on management and in your profession wouldn't hurt. Here is a sample answer:

"I recently read the book Rich Dad, Poor Dad and it was very motivational. It has changed me for the better as I now see challenges as blessings in disguise."

⇥ Describe a circumstance in which your work was criticized

This is a very tricky question that is cleverly designed to get you to confess to a weakness. Everyone has been criticized, so you can't avoid it by claiming otherwise. Begin by stressing the significantly positive feedback you've received during your career, and that you have maintained uniformly excellent performance reviews (if it is true). Here is a sample answer:

"When I was making a logo for one of our clients, my superiors kept on rejecting my ideas. According to them, they were imperfect. That pushed my creativity to a point where I created one of the best logos ever produced by our company."

⇥ What outside interests do you have?

You don't want to come off as a drone, but rather a well-rounded person. However, you don't want to have too much extracurricular activity that will interfere with your job performance. Try to evaluate how the culture of this company would perceive your favorite hobbies, and guide yourself accordingly. Here is a sample answer:

"I enjoy swimming and Yoga. They clear my mind from the hectic activities and reenergize me. I am also the head of our church committee which helps me to perfect my interrelationship skills."

⇥ The fatal flaw question

If the interviewer has reviewed your resume thoroughly, he/she may try to focus on a fatal flaw on your candidacy, perhaps the fact that you have been out of job for a while, or you don't possess a college degree. The secret is to avoid responding in an overly defensive manner. Every salesperson knows that there is always a risk of objections in every sale. The secret is to diminish the anxiety of the buyer, as opposed to exacerbating it. Here is a sample answer:

"I am not perfect but I'm willing to learn and work hard on my weak areas. I have an eye for success, and it's my goal to do everything to the best of my ability."

⇥ What are your thoughts about reporting to a younger person (woman, minority, etc.)?

You greatly appreciate a company that promotes and hires only on merit, and greatly admire that philosophy. You wouldn't certainly be bothered by the age, race, or gender of the person you'd be reporting to. Here is a sample answer:

"I believe that companies hire people out of merit and not by age. I would have no problem reporting to a younger person, as I will be confident that he/she is more experienced and knowledgeable enough to lead me."

⇥ Confidential matters...

This is a relatively simple situation. Restrain from revealing anything confidential concerning a former or present employer. Feel free to explain your reserve diplomatically. Explain that, while you would certainly want to open up as much as you possibly can, you'd also want to respect the wishes of those who've entrusted you with their most confidential information. Here is a sample answer:

"I know how important it is for me to respond to your questions openly, but I'm afraid I can't answer the question about my boss. It is confidential, and if there is one thing that I value the most, it is TRUST."

⇥ Would you tell a lie for the firm?

This question tends to contradict two significant values: integrity and loyalty. Avoid placing yourself in a situation where you have to choose between 2 values by presenting a positive statement that covers all the bases instead. Here is a sample answer:

"I am a principled man, but I also believe that I should protect my company from anything that may try to paint its image in a negative light."

⇥ Would you do anything differently in your life, when you look back?

This question is often meant to reveal life influencing problems, disappointments, regrets, or mistakes that might be related to your performance and personality. Indicate that you're fulfilled, happy, optimistic, and generally wouldn't change anything. Here is a sample answer:

"To be honest, all I can see when I look back, are the terrible mistakes and bad decisions which have made me who I am today. So, No, I wouldn't have it any other way."

⇥ Would you have done better in your previous position?

Avoid falling into this trap of confessing about any minor or major problems. The rule is to avoid being negative. Describe an event that suffered mainly because of external conditions that were beyond your control. For instance, describe how disappointed you felt when a merger, new product launch, or test campaign that looked promising at first, ended up with underwhelming results. Here is a sample answer:

"Looking at my years back as a transport manager, I always did my work with zeal, commitment, and hard work. It earned me some praise from my peers and my manager, but I always felt like I could have done better at the end of the day. There is a lot to learn, and there is always room for improvement."

➤ Are you productive under pressure?

This is a relatively simple question, but your answer needs to be believable. Just say absolutely, and then prove with one or two projects or goals you accomplished under severe pressure.

"Absolutely yes; most recently I had to come up with a new software for my company, and I was given a few days to deliver. I didn't think it was possible, but the pressure motivated me, and I delivered my best work to date."

➤ What triggers your anger?

Be careful not to come off as either a wimp or a hothead. Present an answer that is tailored to the management style of the company and your personality. This is where your research about the company and its management style will come in handy when choosing your words. Here is a sample answer:

"I usually don't get angry easily, but when I do, it comes in the form of people who get in the way of me and my work. I'm very passionate about what I do, and my anger disappears completely when I'm around like minded co-workers."

➤ At this level of your career, why aren't you earning more?

You don't want them to think that you are not interested in money, but you also have to explain why you are earning slightly below your industry standards. Just say that you love to make money, but consider other factors to be more important.

"My dream has always been to change the lives of my clients through repairing their cars. That may be my primary purpose, but I also need my efforts to be well rewarded. Part of the reason I applied for this position is because I can do what I love and get better pay."

✈ Who is your inspiration in life, and why?

Here, the 2 traps are irrelevance and unpreparedness. Struggling to find an answer gives the impression that you have never been inspired, while rambling about your basketball coach in high school is wasting an opportunity to display qualities of excellent value to the firm.

Have some heroes at your fingertips, including your inspirational "Board of Directors" – significant leaders in your line of work. Here is a sample answer:

"My economics lecturer DR. Wayne Smith has been my inspiration and my role model. He taught me how to fearlessly face the business world by believing in myself and the product I am selling."

✈ What's the hardest decision you have ever had to make?

Don't be trapped into giving an irrelevant or unprepared answer. Prepare in advance with an appropriate example, describing how the choice was hard… the process it took… the effective or courageous way you undertook it… as well as the positive results. Here is an example:

"Two years ago, I found myself in a dilemma. I got a marketing job in a good company; the only problem was that I was passionate about being a Chef. I was running short of capital, and taking the job was the logical thing to do. I declined the job and five months down the line, I finally got my cooking job."

✈ What is the most boring job you have ever had?

Describing a very boring job in detail might present a permanent association of you and the boring job in the mind of your interviewer. Just say that you have never permitted yourself to get bored with any job, and you are completely unaware of how others allow themselves to fall into that trap. Here is an example:

"I have always had a positive attitude in everything that I do. My school of thought dictates that whenever you think of a job as boring, you seek out a challenge. That's why I find something interesting in everything that I do."

➤ **Ever spent more than a few days away from work in any position?**

If you have ever had a problem, you could be discovered easily if you lied. On the other hand, admitting you had an attendance problem might raise several red flags. If otherwise, emphasize your consistent and excellence attendance record in the course of your career. Here is an example:

"I have had a good run as far as job attendance is concerned. I have never gone beyond my sick days or my personal days. I am also very flexible to a point that I can repay by working extra hours."

➤ **If you were hired, what changes would you bring?**

Be careful! This question can sabotage your candidacy quicker than a time bomb in a car. Before you make any move, make sure that you are very familiar with everything that the firm is doing in order to make any recommendations. Here is an example:

"If you hired me as the manager for transport in your company, I would, first of all, educate myself on the areas that your buses cover currently. Then, I would try to come up with a way of expanding our horizons by deploying more buses in new areas."

➤ **It is our concern that you don't have enough experience in...**

This could be a determinant question. Chances are the interviewer likes what he/she sees, but is doubtful of a particular area. You may very well have the job, if you can convince them on this point. Before you get into the interview, review your candidacy, and try to spot any weak aspects from the company's perspective. Then you can prepare with the best possible answer to prop up your defenses. Here is an example:

"It is true that I do not have experience in advertising, but I'm a quick learner. I am willing to do whatever it takes in order to fully catch up with my colleagues as I aim higher."

➤ **What are your thoughts about working weekends and nights?**

If you have a family, just say that you are completely comfortable with this type of schedule, and that your family is okay with it. In fact, they are happy for you because they are aware that your work is your greatest satisfaction. Here is an example:

"I have no problem working at night. In fact, that's the best time for me to concentrate. I will be delighted to put up more hours, if that's what it takes to improve the company. However, for me to be 100% productive, I will need some resting time; so if I can't have the weekends, I will have to replace them with one of the weekdays."

✈ Would you be willing to travel or relocate?

Presenting a negative answer would be an end to the interview. Start by finding out the travel cost involved, and the location you'd be required to shift to. If you have no problem, agree enthusiastically. Here is an example:

"I love the adventure that comes with travelling and relocating. For me, it is an opportunity for a fresh start and dealing with a new challenge. I can effortlessly adapt in any environment, and I'm always ready to relocate."

✈ Do you have any experience firing people? Are you comfortable with firing people?

This may seem like an innocent question, but it could very well be the deal breaker. Why? Because the main objective is to unveil poor judgment in hiring that has resulted in you firing so many people. On the other hand, firing so frequently could mean that you are a tyrant. As such, instead of boasting of how many people you have fired, prepare to explain why you had no control over the matter, as opposed to foul temperament or poor hiring procedures. Describe the sensible and rational management process followed during hiring and firing. Check this example:

"Yes, I have, but I wouldn't say that firing people is one of my favorite things to do. Workers are important to a company but that changes when they start being a liability. I have no problem with firing people, especially if it's in the best interest of the company."

⤳ Is there a reason why you've had so many jobs?

The interviewer is concerned that you will leave the position prematurely, as is the case with the others. He is worried that you might be a problem person, or unstable and cannot get along with other people. Try to limit your picture as a job hopper before you even get to the interview stage. Consider getting rid of the less significant entries in your resume, and try to specify the time you took in previous positions in years, as opposed to years and months. Here is an example:

"I choose to look at my last two jobs as stepping stones that taught me what I know today. I can now pride myself on having a wide range of knowledge that is perfect for this position."

⤳ What, in your opinion, is the proper mission/role of a good…? (job title you are seeking)

These types of questions are designed to test how well you understand your position in the broader perspective of your profession, community, company, and department. Consider the most significant ingredients for success in relation to the individual categories mentioned above – your company's role, your responsibility as a manager, your job title, etc. Here is an example:

"As a teacher, my role is to make sure I educate and take care of my students. I am the pivot for education. My mission is to make sure the kids succeed in everything that they are doing.

⤳ How would you tell your boss that an idea he is obsessed with is idiotic?

This question pits 2 values as well: honesty and loyalty, against each other. Keep in mind that in any conflict of values, always go with integrity. Here is a sample answer:

"I would, first of all, hear him/her out and suggest we take time to improve the idea by researching more about it. I will then present to him all the facts and hope he will realize it's a bad idea."

➣ Is there any way you could've enhanced your career progress?

This is another question that is meant to lure you into rewriting your history. There is no winning if you do. Just say that you are overly happy with the progress of your career. Perhaps, if you had prior knowledge earlier in life, which would have been impossible to decipher at the time, you could have shifted to a different direction sooner. Here is a sample answer:

"I believe improvement is a continuous process. My determination and dedication to work hard makes me put myself out there more and constantly learn new things as I improve my skills, which I can later implement to the advantage of the company."

➣ How would you respond if a fellow executive was not pulling his or her weight and was subsequently affecting your department?

These types of questions are meant to test your experience in human relations, as well as how you'd deal with office politics. Try to assess the political style of the company, and respond accordingly. Here is a sample answer:

"I would avoid clashing head on with him/her by using my good communication skills to air out my opinion in a positive way. I would try, as much as possible, to understand them and try to engage in a constructive argument that will make us reason out the issue together."

➣ You have been working at your company for long. Wouldn't it be difficult moving to a new firm?

The concern here is that you are an old dog that'll find it challenging to learn new tricks. You can deal with this objection by highlighting several instances that you have grown and adjusted to varying conditions at your former or present company. Describe the different roles you have had, as well as the wide range of new situations you have faced and dominated. Here is a sample answer:

"Absolutely not, in my previous company, I was once transferred to India to market our new product. I never thought I would have made it, but I managed to know a little bit of their language and coped just fine. That made me stronger, and I don't think there is any type of change I can't overcome now."

➤ Is it okay to refer to your present employer?

This may be the last thing you want, if you are trying to maintain a level of privacy in your job search. However, failure to cooperate might make it seem like you are hiding something. Just express your concern about the need to keep things private, but that it will be completely fine in time. Here is a sample answer:

"My current employer is not aware of this interview; so I will prefer you not contacting him, unless that's the final stage of your employment."

➤ Can you give an example of your creativity (managing ability… analytical skill, etc.)?

You don't want to be caught unawares here. Remember to memorize a list of your most significant and recent achievements, and prepare to shoot them when needed. Here is a sample answer:

"When I used to work at the Smith hardware, I managed to make software which simplified the owner's work of record keeping. That was 5 years ago, and they still use it. Recently, I was part of the team that discovered the software that operates in some of the chain stores around the city of New York."

➤ Any place you could need some improvement?

This is another trick to lure you into admitting weaknesses. Do not fall for the trap. Maintain positivity, like with all the other questions. An excellent way to handle this question is to identify a radical branch in your profession that you would be interested to explore more over the next 6 months (preferably out of your interviewer's needs). Here is a sample answer:

"I am confident with my ability to carry out my day-to-day activities. However, I would love to upgrade my financial skills by taking an advanced class which will enable me to do more for you as a company."

⇥ What are your worries?

Admitting to worrying could make you seem like a loser, while the reverse doesn't sound dependable. Rephrase the term "worry" to avoid reflecting negativity on your portfolio.

"I don't have a worry per se; all I know is that I'm very determined, and I sometimes overwork myself to see a project through. I am currently working on how to give myself a break and still work efficiently."

⇥ What are your usual working hours per week?

Try not to provide a specific number. If you are a workaholic, and feel like this might work in your favor, just say that you are an established workaholic, and that you usually work on the weekends and at night. Your family is comfortable with this as it makes you feel accomplished. Here is a sample:

"I am the kind of person who goes above and beyond to see a project through. This sometimes means me squeezing some extra time of work. My work schedule allows me to work hard from Monday to Friday then rest on the weekend. But I'm open to bend my rules occasionally and come in on the weekends if need be."

⇥ What is the hardest part of being … (job title)?

If you present your answer wrongly, the employer might perceive this to be your weakness. Redefine difficult as challenging, in order to appear more positive, and then identify a part in your profession that everyone finds challenging, but you excel in. Here is an example:

"The hardest part of being a customer care executive is dealing with difficult customers. This separates the real customer cares from the amateurs. It is a very common thing in my field of work, and my 10 years of experience has taught me how to deal with it."

⇥ The hypothetical problem

In some cases, the interviewer might describe a challenging situation and ask how you would handle it. Since such a brief presentation is probably inadequate to produce all the required facts, do not try to solve this problem and give your verdict immediately. Rather, describe the methodical and rational process you'd follow to analyze the problem, the people you'd consult with, brainstorming possible solutions, selecting the best action to take, and observing the results. Here is an example that entails a colleague stealing.

"My moral code will never allow me to just keep quiet when someone is stealing. I will report to the relevant people because I am committed to this company, and I will not condone anything that works against it."

➤ What's the hardest challenge you have ever encountered?

If you are prepared, this is a relatively easy question. Prepare a recent example in advance that displays either:

*A quality that's ever in demand, like intelligence, persistence, courage, persuasiveness, managerial skill, initiative, leadership, etc.

*A quality that's most relevant to the job in question.

Here is an example:

"The toughest challenge I have ever encountered is when I went to a foreign country to study. I did not know their language, and I almost broke down into depression after the first week. I later decided to face my challenges, and I learned their language and started making friends. After 1 year, I was feeling at home."

➤ Ever considered starting your own business?

An affirmative answer here could make you look like a loose cannon, someone that's too entrepreneurial to play as part of a team. On the other hand, a negative answer might make you seem like a security minded drone that has never had a big dream. The best approach is to gauge the corporate culture of the company before giving your answer, and be honest. Here is a good example:

"I am very ambitious, and that thought has crossed my mind a couple of times. But currently starting my own business is not an option for me. I am trying to perfect my art as an employee as I gain more knowledge about the food industry."

⇥ What goals/ambitions do you have?

Be careful not to be caught unawares or to present very vague generalities. Most executives in a hiring position strongly believe in goal setting. They prefer hiring in kind. Here is a good example:

"My short term goal is to get a job in a reputed company like yours, and my ambition is to be an important asset for your organization. I will do this by working hard in order to climb up into a higher and a respectable position."

⇥ What are your main concerns when hiring people?

Speak your mind. However, weave your answers around the 3 most significant qualifications:

*Will the individual fit in?

*Will the individual do the work? (Inspiration)

*Can the individual do the work? (Qualification)

Here is a good example:

"My main area of focus will be the person's ability to carry out the vacant job that is up for offer. I will check this by going through his/ her qualifications and gauge his or her enthusiasm and passion towards the job as I interview them. Self-motivation will also be an area that I will closely focus on, as I ask about their past challenges and how they overcame them."

⇥ What are your strong points as an employee?

Say that you have the ability to meet even the most absurd deadlines; that you're tenacious; and nothing can stand in your way. If the job in question is particularly weaved around meeting deadlines, you can cite an example or two from your previous experience. Here is an example:

"My desire for a perfect end product motivates me to get my projects done. I am also a problem solver, and I never let anything get in the way of my success. Last year, I was given a project, which was almost impossible for me. I was to bring in 50 clients in 3 weeks for our insurance company. I never thought I had it in me, but I went above and beyond until I accomplished that goal."

> ↠ **How would your family, best friend, favorite boss, etc. describe you?**

Some employers believe that, when describing someone close to you, you are more likely to expose certain character insights (flaws) you might have otherwise preferred to conceal. Here is an example:

"I am confident that my best friend will describe me as thoughtful and knowledgeable because I always remember everyone's birthdays. My boss, on the other hand, would describe me as hardworking since I'm the last person who leaves the office, not to mention my good track record of making deadlines."

> ↠ **Define your management philosophy.**

Most firms look for someone who has the ability and desire to distribute, teach, and delegate work, as well as credit, equally. Generally, you don't want to come off as a pushover or a dictator. You should convey that you have the ability to thrive, should the opportunity arise. Here is an example:

"My philosophy as a manager is to give out clear instructions, then stay back and give my juniors time to perform them. But I will make them aware that my door is always open for anyone who needs my guidance and help as I frequently monitor their progress. I also try my best to reason with my junior colleagues during times of conflicts, and that minimizes the level of bad blood in my department."

> ↠ **How do you define "success?"**

This answer should be balanced, citing both professional and personal examples to avoid coming off as either an obsessive workaholic, or an uncommitted employee. Here is a good example:

"For me, success is managing to use your God-given gifts to produce quality work that will empower your customers, colleagues, and the community as a whole."

⤙ How do you define "failure?"

This question gives the interviewer the chance to explore bad decisions and mistakes. He is looking for a willingness to assume responsibility, a clear review of what went wrong, honesty, and the commitment to prevent future occurrences. Here is a good example:

"To me, failure is the art of being unreliable, insufficient, and ineffective when it comes to performing a particular task. Nobody is perfect, but I believe that the people who possess the aforementioned characteristics resemble a 'closed book' because they lack an open mind to be creative and find ways of doing what they have to do."

⤙ What course would you take, if you were starting college tomorrow?

Prepare to present detailed adjustments you might have made when selecting your course in order to better qualify for this job. However, avoid providing a thesis involving an entire change of hair color, minor, or major. Here is a good example:

"If I were to enroll in a college tomorrow, I would make sure that I would combine my human resource course with some public relations units, which will teach me how to relate with my juniors."

⤙ What lessons did you learn from your internships?

The purpose of this question is to determine how coachable you are. Emphasize how you were able to complement your academic training with the real world experience in your internship. Here is an example:

"I was an intern for three months in one of the leading television stations in the country. I was happy to finally use my skills to help them shoot interviews and shows. I learned how to work under pressure, deal with deadlines and also managed to learn how to properly operate all the equipment in production."

⤙ Which courses did you fail the most?

If you failed in accounting, chances are you are not applying for this type of job. Hopefully, you can say that you did not have enough time to prepare for the exams, as you were busy concentrating on your major. Here is a good example:

"To be honest, I wasn't good at I.T when I was in college. I.T was the course that I failed the most, but this was because I was concentrating on business management more. It was my area of major, and I passed with flying colors."

⇢ Describe your last 3 positions.

This kind of question is designed to trim your resume, point out inconsistencies, establish the far more thorough inquiries to adhere to, and assess your ability to edit your response to suit your skills and experience in relation to the job in question. Here is a good answer:

"I started out 10 years ago as a customer service representative in a leading phone company. I took a sales and marketing course, which earned me my next job at our local Samsung office. I later advanced to my current post which is a project manager in the same company."

⇢ Describe the worst/best boss you've ever had

Avoid venomous accusations. Complaining about a boss that was always on your case might present doubt about your reliability to complete a task on time, on budget, or accurately. Here is a good example:

"I have learned a lot from every boss that I have come across. With that being said, my first boss was the best boss I ever served. He mentored me into the world of advertisement and always pushed me to do more while discouraging me from ever giving up. He was such an inspiration, and I owe my success to him."

⇢ What's the biggest failure you have had so far?

Look for a failure that happened way back in your career, and that is completely unrelated to the job in question. Here is a good example:

"My biggest failure comes from a very early age in my life. I had taken a cooking class, knowing very well it wasn't my passion. I went on to be employed in a local food chain where I constantly messed up in the kitchen, and 2 months down the line, I was fired. I learned my lesson and started chasing my dream which is filming."

➤ **What types of people do you find challenging to get along with?**

Saying none might make you seem either stupid or evasive. It is advisable to come up with an anecdote – a brief story that uses humor to soften the reasons you did not get along with someone. Here is a good example:

"It's funny how my boss John keeps on referring to me as the clock. This nickname has grown over the years, and it came from me being strict about time. I normally find it hard to get along with people who don't respect time."

➤ **In your opinion, who are our 2 (3, or 5) main competitors?**

This will slowly and painfully expose the shallowness or depth of your research. If you have a clear handle on the position of the company in the industry, and can sufficiently discuss its strengths, weaknesses, and products as compared to the competition, you have a serious chance. Here is a good example:

"It goes without saying that your company is one of the leading companies in the food industry. Your free delivery idea was ingenious, and that put your company in a whole new level. However, there are only two companies who I can say are your main competitors.

Mac Fries has been very keen with putting up a branch or two in every town in our country, hence starting to create a customer base that can be of threat to you. The second company is McDonald's who have come up with an idea of awarding their 15oth customer with a free meal daily."

➤ **Are you an organized person?**

Discuss in detail about what organizational skills you've developed, including delegation, needs assessment, project management, time management, etc., and how they have enhanced your efficiency. Here is a good example:

"I consider myself as a very organized person. Every day, I start by outlining the tasks ahead of me and then organize them according to priority and deadlines. This helps me to produce high quality in my daily assignments."

⤳ Are you a good time manager?

This is a rather conceptual question, which calls for specifics. For example:

"I have a problem with people who don't respect my time; so I am very conscious when it comes to respecting other people's time to. I usually clock in 10 minutes before time to give myself some space to deal with unrelated matters at work. This helps me to fully focus on my work when I start."

⤳ How do you deal with change?

Think of an example of a situation where you encountered a change that led to a positive outcome. Try to reveal how you embraced and adapted to the change, as well as how you flourished. Here is an example:

"About one year ago, my boss decided to post me in a foreign country where I was supposed to continue my duties as a bus driver. From a distance, it looked impossible for me to succeed in a foreign route. I trained my mind to be positive, and within two weeks, I had it all under control and later went on to be the driver of the year. "

⤳ How do you approach important decisions?

At this point, you are probably familiar with the culture of that particular firm, which can help you tailor your answer to match it. Think about the main concerns of the interviewer, and assess whether you'll need to be creative, analytical, cooperative, and so forth. Here is an example:

"I like to look at every possible angle before I make any important decision. That's why I always make sure to consult with my colleagues, then later analyze the issue and make a clear decision."

⤳ Are you good at anticipating problems, or do you simply react to them?

Every manager panics once in a while. However, the best learn to shield themselves by developing the ability to anticipate problems. Here is a good example:

"The 6 years' experience I have had as a project manager, has taught me that anything can happen. I have had to handle deadline change, colleagues getting sick in the middle of a project and tight deadlines. Those experiences have prepared me mentally to deal with any hiccup in my daily routines without panic."

⇥ Do you like playing it safe, or are you a risk taker?

Often, the interviewer is looking for someone who is a little of both. The aim of this question is mostly to unveil intimations of creativity and innovation. Check out this example:

"When I'm doing my projects, I always give them my all, and I occasionally take risks by pushing my clients to invest more in our investment company. With that being said, I know my limits, and I know when to not push my luck."

⇥ What would you do differently, if you were to start your career from scratch?

Unless you are looking for a complete transformation of career, you need to convince the employer that you would not change a thing. You are happy with your career, and would do it all over again if given the chance. Here is a good way to put it:

"My career as a publisher has been nothing short of amazing. The only regret I have is that it took me so long to get here. I had to go through different career changes before I discovered publishing is what I really wanted."

⇥ Do you like working with others or by yourself?

No matter how much you enjoy the interaction at work, there'll always be people you'd prefer not to socialize with. However, certain job situations force you to get along with them and under difficult circumstances. Describe how you have managed to relate well with different kinds of people. Check this example:

"I am comfortable working with a team as I am working independently. However, it's never easy to deal with people since everyone has different characters, and you will need to constantly keep them in check on their time management and the importance of deadlines."

➤ How do you normally deal with conflict?

Check this example:

"I am a very calm person. I prefer approaching a conflict with an open mind so that I can closely analyze the situation as a whole. I like to solve conflicts by reasoning out with the involved parties rather than bursting out in a confrontation."

➤ How do you react when you have a problem with a colleague?

Here is an example:

"I once had a huge problem with my partner in the advertising department. We couldn't agree about anything. He countered every idea I had with his own. I finally decided to hear his ideas out and demanded the same from him. We both saw the strengths and faults of our ideas, and we decided to think together rather than apart, which resulted in a successful project in the end."

➤ How do you inspire people?

An appropriate answer will highlight how it depends on the individual, and then provide one concrete example or two. Check this example:

"I personally like leading by example, and to me that's the best way of inspiring people. In my department, I used to be the only person who came in early until my colleagues starting seeing how I was constantly winning various awards in our company, and soon, they followed suit. Now my whole department has changed for the better."

➤ What skills do you need the most to advance your career?

Express that you are developing a skill that is connected to job that you are applying. Check this example:

"I recently took on the responsibility of being the chairman of our youth group in my church. The post requires you to control and organize all the projects of the church. I feel this new skill will help me carry out my work more efficiently as an event organizer."

> ✈ **Did you introduce new procedures (policies, systems, etc.) in your last position?**

You don't need to be a department head or divisional president in order to answer this. The employer is looking for creativity, industriousness, and caring about the company and its success. Describe the improvements and changes you made in your previous company, and how they helped the organization in terms of improved production, cost savings, and increased profits. Here is a good example:

"In my last post as a sales and marketing manager, I came up with a system of rewarding our new clients with a welcome gift. This idea went on to be very beneficial to our company. It brought us over 100 customers within two weeks, which was a new record."

> ✈ **Have you been in control of approving expenses, budgeting, and regulating departmental progress? Are you experienced in this area?**

Financial responsibility is a sign that the employer can trust you. Admit if you have not had any or many fiscal duties. However, you can always frame your answer in a creative way:

"Honestly, I have never been in a position to regulate the financial progress of our department. However, I have, on numerous occasions, been invited to the budgetary committee to give estimates of what my projects require. These meetings really enlightened me on how to budget my own projects, and now, I do that comfortably."

> ✈ **How do you deal with troublesome subordinates who are becoming part of the problem?**

This is usually asked in different variations. The employer is trying to distinguish between real leaders and managers with a title, as well as to evaluate whether your style will blend well with that of the organization. Here is a good example.

"I usually sit down with a problematic subordinate and try to understand his/her issues through dialogue. I then explain to them the importance of doing what is supposed to be done and the consequences of doing the opposite. If he/she continues, I have no choice but to fire them."

➤ Why do you want to leave your current job?

You don't want to come off as negative, or even worse, badmouth your current employer. Deal with your discontent very carefully. Picture the next optimum move in your career, and act as if you are applying for that position. Here is a good answer:

"I have gained a lot of skills in my current job, and I have reached a stage where I feel that I want to go to the next level. Unfortunately, my current job doesn't offer the kind of challenge I am looking for, and that's why I have applied for this position, which does."

➤ Where does your employer think you are at the moment?

While it may be possible that you were given a notice or are already laid off, chances are you are still employed. Try to schedule your interviews on a vacation or personal day, after work, or during lunch hour. Here is a good answer:

"My annual holiday began two weeks ago; so he currently knows that I'm enjoying my well-deserved holiday."

➤ Describe how your department is organized. In addition, what is the title of your supervisor and his or her responsibilities?

This question is meant to clarify exactly what you do, in essence, to present responsibilities and duties that match your resume and that correspond to the job in question. Your answer should also tie in well with the previous answers concerning your work experience. Here is an example:

"My department consists of I.T. operators, a project manager, and the head of the department. My supervisor is the project manager, whose responsibility is to supervise our projects and motivate us to meet deadlines."

→ **Describe a typical day at your current (former) occupation. How much time do your spend in meetings? On the phone? Working by yourself? With team mates?**

This question is also designed to prove some of the previous statements that you made concerning your duties, responsibilities, and favorite parts of your job. Here is an example:

"I report to work ten minutes before time which is 7:50 A.M. At exactly 8 A.M, I take on the day's duty by starting with the urgent projects as I move on to the less urgent ones. On Fridays, our department holds a meeting in the afternoon for two hours. I only take urgent calls during work, and I don't deal with my personal issues unless I am on a break."

→ **How long have you been searching for a job?**

As long as you have not been laid off or fired, you should always say that you have only started looking. However, if you believe that the employer can find out if you have been on the job market for long, prepare to explain your reasons for not receiving or accepting any offers. Here is a good answer:

"I have always been on the lookout since I felt like I had outgrown my new job and needed to advance. However, I have never gone for a job interview until I saw your irresistible job offer which is exactly what I am looking for."

→ **How come you've not received any offers?**

You are just as picky about landing the right job as he is about finding the appropriate candidate. Avoid whining or revealing that the search is frustrating you. If you have already landed one or two offers, you could say:

"I actually received an offer recently. They offered me more money, but I turned it down because the challenge I was looking for wasn't there."

Note: It is important to be honest, since the next rational question by the interviewer might be:

→ **Which company made you an offer? At what salary and for which position?**

If you lied in the previous question, you are in hot soup now! Most interviewers are pretty knowledgeable about their competitors, as well as the positions they are looking to fill. If you were honest and told the truth, provide the name of the firm to the interviewer. Here is a good example:

"I was offered the position of being the manager of Norfolk Hotel. My starting salary was $5000 a month which was 1000 more than I'm getting now."

> ➤ **Suppose you don't leave your job; how far do you think you'll advance?**

You might reply by saying:

"My main focus has been to land this job because it will offer me the opportunity to do more with my skills. However, I have an excellent relation with my superiors, who have continually reminded me that I'm one of their greatest assets. I believe CHANNEL 56 will one day expand its horizon and give me an opportunity to head a television station in a foreign country because that's what I want."

Whatever the case, it is always advisable to handle your part as though you are in the driver's seat, happily cruising along until you find the most appropriate position to change lanes. You are certainly not interested in alighting at the next stop, regardless of its destination.

> ➤ **If you are pleased with your current job, why do you want to leave?**

You think that your current employer might go out of business unexpectedly, or you are simply leaving because you broke your engagement with a person in the next office. Do not cry on the shoulder of the interviewer. Here is a good way to answer:

"With the way things are going at WEB CONSULTANCE, I see the company going out of business really soon. They lack the power of evolving, and their competitors may soon catch up with them."

→ **If your boss thinks so highly of you, and you have all these complaints about the job/company/boss, why haven't you informed them of your concerns?**

The employer is trying to hang you by your own rope. If you are such an excellent problem solver, how comes you can't even communicate with your boss about the unfavorable changes in the company that are affecting you negatively.

The only way to handle this question is to maintain as much degree of positivity as possible. You could say:

"WEB CONSULTANCE is a public company with a board of directors. I have argued my case of how expanding will benefit the company time and time again, but I was told the same thing. It will take time for the board to decide. One year down the line and still nothing has changed; that's why I am looking for growth elsewhere."

→ **How would your colleagues describe you?**

Obviously, they'd describe you as a good team player who is relatively easy-going. Besides, you have discovered that people can accomplish a lot more when they unite to find a solution, instead of working against each other. Here is a good answer:

"My colleague, John, keeps on telling me how impressed he is with my hard work, determination, and my team spirit."

→ **Describe specific examples of your role at your current or last job to save effort, be more efficient, reduce costs, increase revenues, etc.**

This is directly related to the previous questions regarding your budgetary responsibility and the organization of your current department. Skilled interviewers find it more convenient to divert to a different set of questions after asking the first one or two questions and then get back to the subject later on. It might be easy to be caught exaggerating when your interviewer gets back to the question afterwards instead of following it up right away. Here is a good way to answer:

"Last year, I was in charge of a project which involved travelling to different places for research. I proposed for us to use a 14 seat vehicle instead of the company fueling everyone's cars for travelling. This ended up saving us a lot of money and time."

> ➤ **In your opinion, what does an employer owe an employee?**

Avoid getting into a discussion on the moral responsibility of the employer to his employees. To this end, avoid getting into legal responsibilities. Instead, try to shift back the focus to your positive outlook, and maintain short and sweet answers. Here is a good way to answer this:

"I think an employer should create an environment where his/her employees can succeed in. My mission is to work hard and let my efforts help me get recognized."

> ➤ **Your supervisor emailed you an assignment and left for the week. You have some questions regarding the assignment, but he/she in unreachable. What do you do?**

If there is no practical way to contact your boss, you would summon the courage to approach their supervisor. Obviously, you'd do this in a manner that would not damage the image of your boss by stating that you did not get the chance to review the assignment with your boss before he/she left the office. Since you are not familiar with the procedures of the company yet, you just want to ensure that you do not go wrong with the assignment. Here is a good answer:

"I would approach my supervisor's superior and tell them I, unfortunately, missed the chance to review my current job with my supervisor and then seek help."

> ➤ **The successful candidate will be working with highly trained people who have a long working experience at the company. How will you blend with them?**

You should instill a level of eagerness in your answer, as the new kid who is anxious to learn from the rest. As such, illustrate the fact that, of course, you are bringing certain aspects to the table but also realize that there is a lot that you need to learn from the individuals you will be working with. Here is a good way to answer this:

"I will humble myself and take the opportunity to learn as much I can. At the same time, I will be very keen in spotting situations where I can offer my skills for the betterment of the company."

> ⇻ **Your supervisor demands that you do something in an obviously incorrect manner. How do you respond?**

This question is very tough, so an answer as follows might be appropriate:

"I would try my best to suggest a different way of doing the same thing and hope that he will agree with me. But if he doesn't, I will have to follow what he is saying because he is my leader."

> ⇻ **How much do you know about our company?**

Again, this is where you will find your prior research useful. Throw out a few positive and salient facts about the organization, and wind up by tossing a question that highlights your interest into the court. For instance:

"This company was founded on the year 1990 by David Richardson with a goal of making our town safer by providing homes and firms with security guards. Currently you have over 400 employees, and you are a leading company in the security industry.

You have 10 branches across the country, and your clients range from big firms to private properties owners.

I am interested in helping you achieve your goal of expanding to cover the region in the next 10 years."

> ⇻ **Do you have any questions?**

Whatever you do, never ever answer with a negative. There is no way you can make one of the most significant decisions of your life without wanting to know more. Even if you believe that you are clear on the duties, you need to speak up, otherwise the employer will assume disinterest. And this could very well be the end of your interview, and when you are just about to land the job. Here is a sample answer:

"Is there anything you can tell me about your organization that is not widely known by the public?"

➤ **What is your primary interest about this position and our company?**

You are looking out for the opportunity to sharpen your skills and develop new ones, the opportunity to supervise more people, more opportunities, and more responsibilities of course, in addition to a higher salary. You can also use this time to demonstrate your knowledge about the organization, as well as how your position can contribute in its success.

"I have been observing your company, and I'm interested in your future plans. The head of the I.T. department will give me a chance to advance and manage a large number of people. These new responsibilities will sharpen my skills, as I perfect the art of being a leader."

➤ **What don't you like about our company?**

This is a tricky question. Of course, the idea is to minimize any negative implications. If you have not heard any terrible news, you may enquire about the recent death of a powerful software, or express your wish that the profits of the company were slightly more predictable. Here is a good answer:

"I have done some comprehensive research about your company and I haven't come across anything I dislike. My only question is what made your new passion drink fail?"

➤ **Describe how you managed a problem employee.**

You should prepare for this sort of question by reflecting on some challenging subordinates. Use two to three examples where you handled a problem subordinate. Try to think about how your intervention changed the situation from negative to positive. For example, perhaps your criticism of an employee or advice to that employee resulted in an improved attitude, or it increased their productivity.

When you're answering this question, discuss the original issue you had with the behavior of the employee, describe the strategies that were used in order to bring about change, and then explain the overall effects this had on you and on the employee's performance.

It's important that you remember that an employer is looking for a manager who has the grace to deal with a chronically underperforming staff member who resists change.

While most employees welcome constructive criticism and motivation in order to improve their performance, there are others who don't welcome advice, and they take personal offense to any sort of intervention.

If you've had some past experiences with difficult employees who didn't respond positively to suggestions made by you, then describe how you outlined a reasonable plan for their improvement and share how you handled their continued non-compliance with this plan. Usually, this involves some sort of collaboration with Human Resources and creating a performance plan with a series of warnings, if the employee refuses to comply.

In some cases, you might relate examples where you coached an employee toward a shift to a job that's more suitable for their background, personality, or their skills. Managers who employ this strategy usually save their company the administrative and financially taxing process that's involved in having to fire someone.

➢ Do you prefer to work independently or on a team?

This can seem like a tricky question, and the answer is both. You need to let your potential employer know that you're comfortable working alone or as a team. When you research the company, the mission statement, and the job description, look for similarities to your previous position where there are assignments that require a good deal of independence and research and others where there was a need for a team effort. Let your potential employer know you're comfortable with both scenarios.

If you haven't had experience with both at your previous employment, then you can go as far back as you need to, such as high school. Tell them about how you enjoyed playing a team sport or how you were required to collaborate with your peers for class projects. Let them know that the overall goal of learning to be a team member was invaluable to you. Then, give them examples of how you excelled when you were working alone, too.

⤳ How do you evaluate success?

During interviews, the interviewers might ask something along the lines of how you evaluate success. A question like this one will give your interviewer a sense of your goals, work ethic, and your overall personality.

The key point here is to focus on the job. In your answer, you need to be aware of the type of job that you're applying to. Where a large corporation might put a lot of emphasis on the bottom line, a non-profit is not going to measure success by money but rather, by social impact.

Make sure you complete your research before you go on the job interview. Browse the company's site, research any presence they may have in the news and media, and see if you can find valuable information about their mission statement. Of course, you need to include aspects of your personality in the answer, too. If there's an area where your values overlap the company's values, then make sure you emphasize this in the interview.

However, you also want to make sure the answer is balanced, demonstrating a dynamic focus on bettering your personal performance, furthering the company's mission, and making a positive impact in the company and on society, too.

If you're confused about how to answer this question yet, here are a few example answers.

"I evaluate success in many different ways. At work, it's meeting the goals that are set by my superiors and my fellow employees. It's my knowledge, from speaking with the other employees that this company is renowned for not only rewarding success, but also giving employees the opportunity to improve, too. After work, I like to play soccer, so success on the field is scoring that goal."

"Success is about doing the job correctly and doing it well. I want to be known as someone who does their job to their best ability and tries their hardest to meet their goals."

"I evaluate my success based not only on my work but also on the work of my peers. In order for me to be successful, the team has to achieve both their team and individual goals."

"I evaluate success based on the outcomes of my actions. It's not only the path that you're taking to achieve your success that matters. It's the quantifiable results that matter."

"To me, success is when I've performed well, and I've met all the requirements of the task, knowing that my work has added value to the company I work for and also to my life and the lives of others."

➤ How do you handle stress and pressure?

This is a very common interview question. The interviewer doesn't want to hear that you've never been stressed out because everyone has felt stress at one time or another while they were at work. Rather, the interviewer wants to know if you know how pressure affects you and if you know how to handle it.

 To answer this question properly, you need to provide some specific examples of how you've handled stress well in previous positions. You could also provide examples of times when the pressure actually made you a more productive employee.

The best way you can answer this question is by giving an example of how you handled stress in another job. That way, the interviewer gets a clear idea of how well you work during stressful situations.

Avoid mentioning times when you put yourself in a stressful situation when you didn't need to. For example, don't share a story about a time when you felt stressed because you procrastinated and needed to finish a project quickly.

Focus on a time when you were given more than one assignment or something that was difficult to complete, and you rose to meet the challenge.

You shouldn't focus too much on how stressed it actually made you feel. While you certainly need to admit that stress does happen, emphasize how you handle the stress rather than how it concerned you.

If you can, avoid saying you're stressed out by a situation that is going to be common in the occupation that you're applying for. For example, if you state you're stressed when you're given a ton of projects to do, and you know the job is going to require that you handle many assignments at one time, you'll look unfit for their position.

You may even consider mentioning how a little stress is a helpful motivator for you, too. You can provide examples of times when the stress of a difficult project allowed you to be a more creative and productive individual.

Some example answers to this question include:

"Pressure is actually imperative to me. Good pressure, like having a lot of assignments to work on or upcoming deadlines, allows me to stay productive and motivated. Of course, there are some times when too much pressure will lead to stress, but I'm skilled at balancing many projects and meeting deadlines, which will prevent me from feeling stressed often. For example, once I had three large projects that were due in the same week, which was a lot of pressure for me. Yet, because I made a schedule that detailed how I'd break down every project into smaller goals, I completed all three of them ahead of time and avoided any unnecessary stress."

"I react to the situations rather than to the stress. That way, the situation can be handled and won't become a stress inducer. For example, when I handled an unsatisfied customer, rather than feeling stressed out, I focused on the task in front of me. I believe my capability to communicate well with the customer, during that moment helped reduce my stress, and alleviated that situation and also reduced the stress that the customer was feeling."

"I work better when I'm under pressure, and I've found that I like working in a challenging environment. As an editor and a writer, I flourish under speedy deadlines and handling many projects at once. I discover that when I'm under the stress of a goal, I do some of my most creative work."

➤ How do you plan to achieve those goals?

This is a follow-up to the question of what your goals are for the future. The interviewer will usually ask you how you plan to attain those goals.

A good answer to this question is to speak specifically about what it is you want to accomplish, and how you'll accomplish it. Examples of a good response include:

"I plan to gain additional skills by taking some related courses and continuing my involvement with many professional associations."

"I noticed that this company provides some in-house training for employees, and I'd certainly be interested in taking classes that would be relevant to my position."

"I'll continue my professional development by participating in seminars, conferences, and furthering my education."

> ➤ **If the people who know you were asked why you should be hired, what would they say?**

When an employer is asking you why they should hire you, they're really asking what makes you fit for the position they're offering. Your answer to this question needs to be a concise sales pitch that describes what you have to offer them.

The best way you can respond to this question is to give some concrete examples of why your accomplishments and skills make you the best fit for the position.

Take some time to compare the job description with the capabilities you have, as well as mention what you've accomplished in the other positions you've held. Be positive and repeat your interest in their company and the position at hand. Here's how you can prepare your response.

First, to prepare an answer to this question, take a look at the job description before you go in for the interview. Make a list of the requirements for that position, including any skills, personality traits, and qualifications. Then, you need to make a list of the qualities that you have that fit these requirements.

For every quality, try to think of a specific time that you used that trait in order to achieve something while you were at work.

For example, if you've listed that you're a team player, then think of a time where your capability to work well in a team resulted in a project that was completed successfully.

Second, keep your answer concise. You need to keep the answer brief, no more than a few minutes long. So you should select one or two specific qualities from the list that you've made in order to emphasize your sales pitch of yourself. Start by describing what you believe they're looking for in an employee, and how you fulfill their need.

Third, you need to focus on your individuality. The interviewer wants to see how you are notable amongst the other candidates for the position. Therefore, you should focus on one or two qualities that you possess that might be unique, or a little harder to find in the other candidates. For example, if you're experienced with a certain skill their position requires, then tell them. This is your opportunity to tell them why you'd be an invaluable employee to them.

Take a look at some of the best answers to this question.

"I believe my experience in this industry and my capability to work alone makes me an excellent match for this position."

"I have the experience, know-how, and the excellent communication skills to be an asset to this company."

"Your company provides a lot of services that I've had experience with, in a variety of settings. I believe my familiarity with your industry will make me an excellent fit for this position."

"You've iterated that you're looking for a sales executive who's able to effectively manage over twenty employees. In my ten years of experience as a sales manager, I've developed some strong team-building and motivational skills. I was awarded the manager of the year award twice for my innovative strategies for motivating my employees to meet and surpass their monthly deadlines. If I were hired, I'd be bringing my leadership capabilities and strategies for achieving gains in profit to this position."

"I've excellent administrative skills, and I know I'd be an asset in your office. My skill set is a perfect match for the position you're looking to fill. Also, I welcome the opportunity to work with others, and would welcome the opportunity to be part of your company."

"You describe in your job listing that you're looking for someone who has an abundance of compassion and patience. Having served as a nurse at a nursing home over the summer for the past two years, I've developed a capability to be very patient while still taking care of my patients. My experience with the elderly above the age of fifty-five has taught me strategies for working with all people who are in need with a smile, no matter what. My previous employer would often place me in with the patients who had the most severe of problems because of my history of patience and empathy. I'll bring not only experience to your company, but creative problem-solving skills, empathy, and patience to this position."

> ➤ **If you knew a manager is 100% wrong about something how would you handle it?**

Sometimes interviewers are going to ask you a question about how you handled a situation when your boss was wrong. They might ask you what you did when you knew your boss was wrong, or if you knew your boss was completely wrong about something, how would you handle it? An interviewer is going to ask you this to see how you handle a difficult situation. They will also ask this to see how you view your relationship with your superiors.

Interview questions about your superiors are slippery slopes. You need to demonstrate that you're tactful while you're handling a boss, but you also need to demonstrate that you know when you should point out someone else's errors.

Here are a few tips for answering this type of question.

> ➤ **Do not tell the person it's never happened. The interviewer doesn't want to hear that you've never corrected a boss because this isn't realistic, and it's a sign that you don't think for yourself.**

> ➤ **Use examples if you've handled a situation like this with a former employer.**

➤ Explain what that situation was and how you handled that situation and also tell them the ultimate result. Answering a question like this in a behavioral interview will provide the interviewer with some solid information about how you handle this type of situation, whether it's with a boss or with another employee.

➤ Explain these situations are rare. While you should provide one example of a time that you tactfully told a boss that they were wrong, you need to explain that this doesn't happen often. You don't want to seem like you're the type of employee who's constantly questioning their boss. Ideally, your example should be from a situation that directly affected you and your team's capability to complete a job successfully.

➤ Explain how you told the superior they were wrong. One of the reasons the interviewer is asking this question is to see how tactfully you handled the situation. Therefore, when you're describing the example, you need to emphasize the polite way that you spoke to them. If you made sure to speak them in private, and not in front of other employees, then say so. This shows you're thoughtful, and you think carefully about communication.

➤ Don't talk badly about your former superior. Even if you're noting a mistake your boss made, don't speak negatively about them. Even if you had a lot of complications with them, or they were often wrong, don't tell the interviewer this. Explain that the times when you needed to correct your boss were rare.

➤ Explain the results of correcting your boss. Tell the interviewer the positive results of the conversation that happened. Perhaps your boss thanked you for sharing the information with them. Maybe an error had been corrected, which ultimately helped out the company.

Some sample answers to this question might be:

"The rare few times in the past that I had to speak to a former employer about a particular error, I did it in private. Recently, my superior assigned my team a project, but I knew the data she'd supplied us with was a few years old, and there was more current data out there. Working with the most recent information was vital to the success of our project. I went to my manager's office and spoke to her confidentially about the mistake, simply showing her the most current information. She thanked me and instantly updated that information. We completed our project on time and with a great deal of success."

"Sometimes, in the past, I've spoken to a superior about an error, but only when I thought the error would negatively impact the company I worked for. For instance, a former employer instituted a new online storage system, and they were not aware that the system was not easily accessible on the employee computers. During the daily open office hours my boss held, I privately discussed with him the issue and pointed out the effect these complications have on the employee's capability to complete the assigned tasks. He was so glad I brought up the issue that he put me in charge of fixing the issue, resulting in increased productivity for all the employees."

> ➤ **Share some examples of how you have impacted worker safety.**

Most employers have concerns about worker safety because injuries and other workplace accidents can impact employee morale, productivity, and the company's insurance rates, while also leaving the company vulnerable to lawsuits.

Therefore, it's not a surprise that interviewers ask candidates about their track records when it comes to employee safety, especially when they're interviewing someone for a management position.

The first step to answering this question is to think about the occupation safety and hazards in a comprehensive way. Consider all the possible things that could go wrong and all the threats to the employees in the workplace. Of course, physical safety in construction, production, mining, agricultural, and transportation industries come to mind because accidents are much more common in these industries.

However, you also need to consider health and environmental threats in industries such as research, healthcare, and biotechnology or pharmaceutical industries where exposure to disease and harmful chemicals might endanger the employees.

If you've worked in the typical office environment, these issues might not seem so relevant; however, there are numerous other elements to take into account. For instance, musculoskeletal damage is a possibility when workers do repetitive motions that are awkward or other physically demanding tasks. Improper posture while seated at a desk is also physically detrimental.

You also don't want to forget any psychosocial elements such as emotional stress in industries such as air traffic control, or deadline oriented pressure in industries such as publishing. There are also occupations where employees have to handle the stress of an irate patron or an unruly student. Sexual harassment is another consideration that has a profound impact on the well-being of the employees.

Of course, the little things matter, too, such a drinking, smoking, too much soda or coffee in order to stay awake at work, whether or not the fellow employees are getting exercise and eating healthy, so on. In your answer, you might include something apparently trifling as encouraging a co-worker to take a stroll with you during a break to bring in a homemade, healthy lunch rather than ordering something.

To prepare your answer, the next step is to itemize the actions that you took in order to address any of the threats to an employee in previous work environments. The best approach is to come up with three or more scenarios where you addressed some workplace health or safety issues. Describe the extent of the issue or a baseline status of the worker safety. Then you should outline any steps you took in order to increase the employee's well-being and any impact that your steps had on the frequency or the severity of the issue.

Interventions could take the form of training programs, worker education, workplace safety displays, establishing new procedures and policies, communications campaigns, replacing or repairing machinery, requiring protective gear, barriers or clothing, sanctioning offending staff, rewarding safe behaviors, providing ergonomic devices, or incorporating more breaks into a worker's schedule.

Here are a few example answers to this question to give you an idea of how to respond.

"You can see on my resume that I currently work as a production manager at a car manufacturer company. I discovered shortly after I took the job that there were several hand injuries from one of the bolt machines. I learned from Human Resources that seven employees in the past three years had received medical attention or missed time from work when they were stationed in this area of the assembly line. Human Resources staff had interviewed the workers and believed fatigue had been the contributing factor. I decided to decrease the amount of time between the five-minute breaks from ninety minutes to forty-five minutes, put a safety reminder sign in easy view of the employees, and personally reminded those who were stationed at this area to make sure they were focusing on what they were doing. During the following year, there was only one incident of an employee being injured in that area. I also researched some alternative machines that would perform at the same level with less risk and upper management is considering my proposal at the moment."

If you haven't had the opportunity to increase employee health in the previous workplace, whether it's due to a lack of internal resources or a lack of approval from your superior, you can still utilize this inquiry as a chance to sway your interviewer. If this is the case, then come up with problems you noted and approaches you would have put in place, if you'd have approval. Explaining the situations you observed and the responses you'd come up with shows a level of organizational engagement on your end, which your interviewer will see as an asset to their team.

➤ What applicable qualities / knowledge do you have?

When you're asked questions that relate to the knowledge that qualifies you for the position, it's imperative that you are specific about your skillset and your experiences.

The greatest way to respond to this is to describe your responsibilities in detail and to connect these to the position you're interviewing for. Tie your responsibilities in with those that are listed in the job description for the new position.

That way, your interviewer will see that you harbor the qualifications that are necessary for the position. Focus mostly on your responsibilities that are directly related to the position's requirements.

It's also imperative that you're honest, and you're accurate. Never embellish your position because you don't know when the hiring manager is going to check your references.

Here are some examples of how you can match your qualifications to a job description.

"I actually have similar experience to what you're looking for in an employee. In my current or previous position, I held the duties that I'd have if I were to take on this job."

"I have several years of experience in an office."

"I'm well organized, and I know how to use my time efficiently."

"At my previous occupation, my responsibilities included many of those that are required for this position."

"I'm a bit of a perfectionist when it comes to being efficient. I feel compelled to finish what I start, and I'm punctual."

➔ **What are you looking for in your next job? What is important to you?**

One of the interview questions you could be asked is what you're looking for in your next position. The interviewer would like to know whether your goals match the ones of the company. It's also an excellent way for the interviewer to see whether your interests and skills make you a good candidate for the position they're hiring for.

To answer this question properly, you need to think carefully about your goals and how you can relate them to the position at the company. While your answer needs to be honest, it also should demonstrate how you'll add value to the company.

Here are some tips on how to answer.

→ **When you're preparing for the interview, review the requirements in the job description. Then, you need to make a list of your own goals and interests. Be sure you take note of anything that's on both sides of the paper.**

→ **When you're answering this question, you need to emphasize your goals and interests as they relate to the job. This way, you can offer a more personalized response specifically tailored to the position that you're applying for.**

→ **While the question will ask you to focus on what you want in that position, you should also frame your answer so that you put emphasis on how you are going to benefit the company. For example, you could explain that you would like to work for an organization that encourages team projects and teamwork because you do well in a team environment. This shows the interviewer that you're going to do well in the company's team-driven culture.**

→ **Lastly, make sure you give the interviewer an honest answer. Even though you'd like to show how well you're a good fit for their organization, you shouldn't lie to them. They will be able to tell when your answer is not authentic. Use honest answers that also show you are going to do well at the position being offered.**

Here are a few example answers to get you started.

"I'm looking for a job where I have the opportunity to use my written communication skill set. If I were to be a marketing assistant for your organization, I'd be able to apply my years of experience as a successful grant writer, and I'd be able to write the type of materials I most enjoy working with."

"I'm hoping for a position that'll let me have the chance to boost sales at a company that's already successful, such as yours. I'm looking for the opportunity to use the skills I've developed through my years in marketing to engage your sales force and increase international sales and productivity."

"I'm ecstatic to have the opportunity to work with a successful, innovative company such as yours. I look forward to using the experience I've obtained in technology to help streamline your company's products for even more successful use."

"At my next position, I'd like to be able to have a positive impact on the client, and to be able to help them lead a healthier, more functional lifestyle. Your facility offers a total recovery program for patients, and I feel my education, experience, and specialization makes this an excellent fit for me."

"I look forward to working for an organization that has a mission that I can firmly uphold, such as yours. I look for positions that I am passionate about because this allows me to be creative and productive."

➤ What are your salary expectations?

Before you begin to talk about salary and pay with a potential employer, you have to find out how much the position and you are worth to the company. You'll need to take some time to research the average salary in your area. That way you'll be prepared to obtain what you're worth and to get an offer that's reasonable and realistic.

Salary negotiations involve talking about a job position with a potential employer to negotiate the salary and benefits that will meet your criteria.

Before you begin salary negotiations, you have to know how much the position is worth, try to figure out how much flexibility there might be on the part of the employer, and how you can negotiate a salary for the job you're being offered.

Once you know that you should be earning a certain amount, how do you go about obtaining that amount? Begin by being patient. When you're interviewing for a new position, do your best not to bring up the compensation rate to the employer until they've made you an offer.

If you're asked what your requirements are for pay, say they are open based on the position and the overall compensation package that's available. Or tell them that you'd like to know more about the challenges and the responsibilities of the position before you discuss the salary.

Another option to give them a salary range that's based on the research you've completed up front. Once you've been given an offer, you do not have to reject or accept that offer right away. A simple, "I need to think about this" can get you an increase in their original offer.

If you're unsure about the position, then a "no" can bring you a better offer, too. However, this can backfire if you really need the job. If you absolutely need the job, then you might not want to negotiate too much with salary.

When you're considering a job offer, it's imperative that you know the bottom line, which is how much your net pay is going to be. You can use some paycheck and salary calculators to guess how much you'll bring home in the paycheck.

→ **What can you contribute to this company?**

Often, during the job interview, you'll get a question about how you'll contribute or add value to the organization. This question will give you the opportunity to explain what makes you stand out amongst the other candidates applying for the job, and how you'll be an asset to that organization.

The best way you can answer the questions about your contributions to the company is to give an example of how you have accomplished just that in the past and relate it to what you can achieve in the future.

Here's a little advice on how to answer this question.

Accentuate what you've done in the past and connect it with the future. Give some concrete evidence from past occupations to show how you've contributed to another company. Past examples will show an employer the kind of work that you're going to likely do for them. Describe some specific examples of how effective you've been in other positions, changes that you implemented, and goals that you have attained.

Talk about the breadth and the depth of your related experiences. Yet, you want to conclude by explaining that you'll bring these types of accomplishments to the current company you're interviewing with.

Use some information you've gathered. Interviewers ask this question because they want to know how much value you'll add to their company. To demonstrate this, you may want to use some numbers to show how you added value to a company in the past. For instance, did you increase a company's sales records? If so, how much? Did you raise a certain amount of funds for a company? Numbers will show concrete evidence of how you've contributed to a company, and how you'll likely contribute to a company in the future.

Be sure you connect your answer to the interviewer's goals. Whatever example you decide to focus on, be sure it's related to the specific job or the company you're going for. You'll want to let the interviewer know you have the skills that are necessary to complete the job they're hiring for, the capability to effectively meet their challenges, and the diplomacy and flexibility to work well with others and with your superiors. If there are specific skills or qualities that are especially important for this position or this company, then you should focus on them.

Here are a few example answers to get you started.

"I can add my capability to streamline office process. As an example, I created a new method to schedule client appointments, which led to an eighty-five percent decrease in errors in scheduling. I would like to bring not only this method but my organization skills, to this position at your organization."

"I'll bring my unique vision to your organization. I'm experienced in numerous areas related to this company's current aspirations, including expanding international sales. As an example, I helped improve the international sales at my previous company by over twenty-five percent. My sales background, along with my capability to plan ahead, is going to help facilitate that growth."

"My previous background at my previous company included innovation in numerous different areas, including strategies for better teamwork. At the organization I worked for before, I created strategies to improve communication and teamwork amongst the members of team projects. I am able to bring not only my ideas from my previous position but my general passion for innovating to your company.

➤ What can you do for this company?

This is a common interview question that's used to figure out what assets you have that will be specific to the company's goals.

First, you need to be sure that you've researched the company before the interview so that you're familiar with the company's goals. Respond by giving some examples of your skills, education, and accomplishments, and your experience that will show that you would be a good asset for the organization.

Take some time to compare your objectives and goals of the company and the position, as well as mention what you've accomplished in your previous jobs. Be positive and repeat your interest in the company and the position they're offering.

➤ What do people most often criticize about you?

Employers ask this question to find out how sensitive you are and how well you accept constructive criticism. The interviewer might ask you this question as a way to discover any red flags or qualities that would make you a bad candidate for the position.

Here's how you should answer.

Be careful about answering this question. You don't want to suggest that you're criticized all the time on the job, but you also don't want to suggest you're perfect at your job. It makes sense to mention things that aren't specifically related to the job that you're applying for. You want to emphasize that the criticism or the weakness doesn't affect your capability to perform your job well.

You should also mention a flaw that might actually be considered an asset for this position. For example, you could say that certain people have alleged you're too critical of your work, but you can clarify that you have a strong attention to detail, and you carry that attention to detail to your workplace.

The best type of answer is going to explain how you improved on a weakness that you once had. This is going to demonstrate that you're excellent at taking criticism.

Here are a few example answers to this question.

"There's no continuous criticism. I'm open to professional and personal growth and welcome the opportunity to improve myself."

"One of the things that I'm sometimes accused of is being too much of a perfectionist. I have a tendency to expect high standards of work from myself."

"A few years ago, I had a supervisor who told me that I was too critical of others' work. I took that seriously and made sure that, from that point on, my analysis and my suggestions were always supportive and helpful rather than critical. In recent events, people have praised my capability to give useful and thoughtful feedback."

"From the moment I was a child, I always had a hard time presenting things in a group setting. A few years ago, I took some courses pertaining to public speaking, and last year I attained an award for a presentation that I gave at the company's annual executive board meeting."

If humor's appropriate, this would be an excellent time to use it. But remember, keep in mind that the interviewer might press you for a more serious answer, so you should have one ready.

> ➤ **What do you expect from a manager?**

This question is going to determine how well you're going to work with your superiors. You need to be honest here, but also be tactful. Some example answers might include the following.

"I appreciate work environments where my manager tries to make a personal connection with the employees."

"In my previous occupation, I enjoyed the fact that management didn't show favoritism, and they understood the employee's needs, as well as their strengths. Of course, these things will take some time to know, but I would like my superior to try to know me in this way."

"I would like to be able to go to a manager if I had an issue or an idea and be able to feel comfortable expressing what I felt to him or her. I would also expect a superior to be honest and open with me and to inform me if there was anything I could do in order to improve myself or do differently."

→ **What do you find are the most difficult decisions to make?**

There are not really any right or wrong responses to a question like this. The interviewer just wants to see that, when you've faced a difficult situation or decision, you were able to handle that situation. They also want to see what type of decisions you consider hard.

These are behavioral interview questions that are designed to figure out how you're going to handle a certain situation. The logic behind them is that how you behaved in the past is a prediction of how you're going to behave in the future.

When you're answering this type of question, give a few concrete examples of some difficult situations that you had to handle while you were at work. Then discuss what decisions you needed to make to remedy the situation.

You want to come across as being capable and confident of making your decisions. Avoid any examples that make you seem uncertain or indecisive.

In addition, keep the answers you give positive. Such as, "even though it was a difficult decision to lay off that person, I did so in a professional manner, and this decision led to improvements in productivity and efficiency in the department." Whatever answer you provide, make sure you're specific. Itemize what it was that you did and how you accomplished it.

The best way to prepare for this type of question, where you'll need to recall an event or an action, is to refresh your memory. Go through your resume and reflect on some specific situations you had to handle or projects that you were working on. You can use these in order to create a response. Prepare some stories that will demonstrate the times when you successfully solved a difficult situation.

Here are some examples of answers to this question.

"Decisions I've made within a team were difficult, but only because they took more time and required deliberate communication between the team members. As an example, I worked on a team project where my colleagues and I had to make a few choices about how to use a limited budget. Due to these decisions involving some group discussions, our team learned how to communicate well with each other, and I believe we made the best decision for the team because of that."

"Being the manager, the most difficult decision I needed to make involved layoffs. Before I made those tough decisions, I always tried to think carefully about what is best for the organization and the employees. While I don't enjoy making these types of choices, I don't shy away from this part of my position. A few years ago, I needed to let some employees go because of the economic climate. This decision was hard for me and was ultimately necessary for the good of the organization and everyone working for the company."

➤ **What major challenges and problems did you face? How did you handle them?**

The question of how you handled challenges is a difficult one. On one side, it's the opportunity for you to communicate your problem-solving and critical thinking skills, along with your aptitude to succeed under a stressful situation.

However, on the other side, there are many ways you can handle a challenge. One company could favor an employee who takes some measured, procedural and deliberate methodology, where another organization might prefer someone who dives in and does all that they can in order to meet the challenge without really thinking about the larger picture.

This is a pretty tricky question, so how should you answer it?

Before you take a look at some sample answers, let's review the process for arriving at the best response. After all, you're not going to have these sample answers with you at the interview, so you have to be able to come up with your own answer on the spot.

Think about a challenge that was significant but one that you considered to be successful. Most importantly, you also want to be able to talk about a real professional challenge and not an annoying or an arbitrary occurrence. You also have to be able to elaborate on how you met the challenge successfully. If you can, mention a challenge that's most relevant to the role that you're applying for.

Don't just tell the interviewer what you did, but explain how you did it. The interviewer is interested in learning how you approached the situation, including the actions that you took and your thought process as you took them. Don't skip into the future to the end result. Use some specifics to describe what you did in order to contribute to the answer.

Emphasize the outcome of your actions, and what you learned from the situation. The interviewer wants to hire someone who can turn a challenge into an opportunity. When you're brainstorming an answer, think about the ways you can highlight how you made the most of a difficult situation. Of course, in reality, it's not possible to wave your magic wand and transform all difficult challenges into successes. However, it's possible to learn from mistakes and hardships, and then apply your knowledge to future situations. Be sure you express what you learned and how you grew from handling that challenge.

Here are a few example answers to this question.

"During a difficult financial situation, I was able to satisfactorily negotiate some repayment schedules with vendors. I created an equally beneficial imbursement plan and barter program that worked with the company's cash flow and project schedule and the vendor's needs at the same time. Also, the agreement was easier for me to obtain because I worked hard with developing a positive relationship with the vendors in the months that we worked together. From this experience, I learned the importance of thinking outside of the box and solving situations that weren't ordinary. I also learned the importance of creating and maintaining positive relationships with vendors."

"When the development of software of our new product halted, I coordinated the team and managed to get the schedule back to where it needed to be. We were able to troubleshoot the issues successfully and solve the problems in a short period of time, and we didn't completely burn out the team in the process. I did this by incentivizing the senior engineering team to come up with an innovative technology solution that would solve customer's issues with fewer development hours on the company's end."

"A long-term client was threatening to take their business elsewhere. I met with them and was able to change how the account was handled on a daily basis, in order to keep their business. From this complication, I learned the importance of being aware of client relationships, and operations not just after the issues arose, but for the duration of the business relationship. As a result, other account managers adopted the process I used and have also seen improved results with their accounts, too."

➤ What motivates you?

When you're applying for a position, one of the most common job interview questions is something along the lines of what motivates you. This is an open-ended and broad question that can make it difficult to know how to answer. Most people are motivated by numerous factors, such as prestige, pay, making a difference, interacting with others, and seeing results.

When an interviewer asks this question, they are hoping to figure out what makes you tick. An honest answer will help reveal what circumstances will allow you to feel enthused and excited. Another common variant is asking what you're passionate about. Giving insight into the things that motivate you at work will show the interviewer your personality and your working style, and help give them a sense of how you are as a person and as an employee.

After all, there's big difference between someone who is motivated by building a team and establishing a strong relationship with their peers and the candidate whose best day involves working on a report that improves the company's cash flow.

Both of these candidates will bring strong advantages, and this question helps interviewers narrow down the person that's the best fit for the position and the company.

So how do you answer this question?

When you answer the question, you need to be honest, but also keep the audience in mind. While you might be most motivated by receiving a regular paycheck, that answer isn't very inspiring from the interviewer's perspective. It's hard to think of a decent answer for this question right on the spot since it requires some self-reflection.

To prepare an answer, think about the jobs that you've had in the past. What happened during the best days? What were you most looking forward to on your days at the office? When did you come home from work with stories and feeling excited and enthusiastic?

Whether it was a successful meetup with a client or a complex project that was dealt with, keep everything in between in mind when you frame an answer. In addition, consider the skills and capabilities calls for. If you're applying to be a manager, then framing your answer around relationship-building capabilities and helping those around you succeed and meet their goals could be a stronger answer than a discussion about learning something new or working with new clients.

Some example answers to this question might be the following.

"I want to be part of a team that has a lot of intelligent people who have interesting ideas."

"It excites me to work with clients on a personal level, and to see positive results from those relationships."

"I enjoy preparing and giving presentations. Being up in front of an audience and seeing how they respond to my ideas is an amazing thrill for me, and making that connection is exciting and inspiring."

"I'm highly driven by results. I enjoy it when I have a concrete goal to meet and enough time to figure out a strong strategy for accomplishing it. At my previous occupation, the yearly goals were quite aggressive, but I worked with my team and my manager to figure out a month-to-month strategy in order to meet the year-end goals. It was an amazing thrill to meet that goal."

"I'm motivated by digging down into the data. If you give me a spreadsheet and some questions, I'll be eager to figure out what's driving those numbers. In my current position, I prepare the monthly analytics report around the sales. The information from these reports helps determine and drive how the company charts their next steps and makes sales goals for the following months, and having that influence, and providing the important information, is very motivating for me."

"Learning something new has always been an excellent motivator for me. From every occupation I've had the pleasure of having, I believe I've continually been able to learn something new, or a new way to solve a problem."

"I'm highly deadline-driven and enjoy having the opportunity to figure out the new organizational system that'll help keep me on track in order to meet the deadlines."

"I really enjoy providing coaching and mentoring to my peers. I'm everyone's go-to person when they need a question answered, or they need another opinion, and I'm always happy to help them out."

"I was responsible for many projects where I directed development teams and put into practice repeatable processes. The teams achieved a hundred-percent on-time delivery of the software products. I was motivated by the challenge to finish the projects ahead of time and by managing the teams that achieved the goals."

"I've always wanted to ensure my company's clients get the best customer service that I'm able to provide. I've always felt that it is imperative, for both me personally, the company, and the clients, that I provide a positive customer experience. My drive to constantly grow my customer service skills is the reason that I earned top sales at my company for an entire year."

"I've always been motivated by the desire to meet deadlines. Setting and reaching the deadlines gives me an enormous sense of accomplishment. I enjoy making an organized schedule to complete a task and achieve my deadlines. For instance, when I ran a fundraising event the previous year, I set many deadlines for numerous tasks that led up to the event. Achieving all the deadlines motivated me to keep going, and made the event run very smoothly."

➤ What strategies would you use to motivate your team?

Employers are usually interested in assessing how well a co-worker and client will respond to you if you were hired, and how you'd interact with them. Therefore, you should prepare for questions about how you'd motivate a team.

Here's how to respond to this question.

One of the imperative dimensions of your interpersonal style is your method for motivating others, especially if you'll be directing staff, handling projects, or leading teams of peers.

In addition, you might encounter this form of questioning while you're interviewing for jobs in public relations and sales, where you need to motivate a client or customer.

There are different motivation strategies for different types of people. While there are a variety of ways you can answer this question, ultimately, you need to convey your understanding that there are different approaches that will work for different types of people. A good beginning point is to mention you would take the time to get to know your clients or your team members, and assess their needs and their preferences.

It's also helpful to differentiate how you might approach staff who are performing well versus the underperformers of the office. Like any other situational interview question, you should provide a specific example of how you motivated someone in your previous roles.

If you're interviewing for a position in public relations, sales, fundraising, or marketing, where you need to convince someone to participate in some manner, you need to share how you learn about their needs and preferences. Then you can mention how you'd emphasize the benefits of your services or products in light of those desires and needs, in order to get the desired response from them.

Here are some example answers for you to review.

"When it comes to motivating others by recognizing achievements, I believe that recognizing the good aspects of their performance is critical to motivating most employees. For example, I managed a staff of ten employees and noticed one of them was a little introverted and tended to stay in the background. She performed well but was reluctant to contribute during meetings, and I thought she could be more productive if she was optimally motivated. I began a daily ritual of checking in with her and monitoring her output. I provided her with some positive feedback for her daily achievements, and I discovered the quantity and quality of her output increased when I interacted with her more often. I was able to call on her at meetings because I understood the details or her work better and asked her to share some of her successful strategies with her colleagues."

"When it comes to motivating others by giving them consistent feedback, I believe regular and tangible feedback is imperative when handling a worker who's not performing equal to his or her potential. I overheard grievances from some restaurant customers that one of the bartenders was not as attentive and cheerful as they would have preferred. I began asking her customers as they left about the quality of service and informed her as soon as I could after they left about what I'd learned. I let her know that her actions were challenging and praised her when the customers were content. After a few shifts, her attitude changed, and she began to receive consistently positive feedback from customers."

"When it comes to motivating others by establishing a context for their work, I believe staff is highly driven when they comprehend the impact of their role in a project. I also believe they are more likely to be driven if they have some say concerning how to achieve the department or group goals. When I launched a campaign for fundraising for a new library, I called a meeting to clearly outline the purpose of the drive and how it would benefit a college. Then I asked the members to share their insights regarding the best process for achieving the goal. After we had brainstormed some strategies to get the best results, I drew a consensus around a plan and designated the responsibilities for every team member. The group was invested in this campaign more than in some of their past efforts, and we attained our goal ahead of schedule."

"When it comes to motivating others in sales, I know how to motivate. As you can see from my resume, I've sold accounting software in the past. My approach to motivating the potential customers was to spend some time discovering the challenges and problems that challenged their development staff. Then I'd pitch features of my product that would help them overcome these problems. For instance, I met with one museum development officer and discovered they did not have a systematic way to process their accounts receivable. The staff relied on some handwritten documents and bills collected in the mail. I showed the development officer how our software processed the accounts receivable in one location, and he decided to purchase a lease once he saw how the system could help the staff focus on how to complete the rest of their job without having to worry about finding all the documentation."

✈ What was it like working with your manager?

One of the typical interview questions is "what was it like working with your boss." The reason this question is asked is because it's used to find out how you got along with your superiors. Be careful about how you answer this question. Interviewers do not like to hear too much or much at all about how bad a boss was because it might be someone from their company that you're talking about the following time around.

✈ What was most / least rewarding?

Interview questions about what was the most rewarding and the least rewarding are a little tricky. You need to be sure that the thing you're saying is least rewarding does not involve the responsibilities that will be a major part of the position you're interviewing for.

As an example, if the last job you had involved some extensive customer service phone skills that you hated, and if being on the phone doing something similar is even a minor part of your new job, don't mention it. Rather, focus on the tasks that were most rewarding and highlight them instead.

You need to match the response to the job. When you're interviewing, be aware of the job that you're interviewing for and be sure to tailor your response to it. Try to accentuate the positives, regardless of what question has been asked because you don't want to be seen as someone who is negative about working in general.

You also need to take the time to make a list of the qualifications that the employer is looking for and be sure the responsibilities that you mention as being the most rewarding match that list.

When you're asked about what was the least rewarding, mention something that isn't required in the new job. Again, keep it as positive as you can. You could frame it as something that was the least rewarding compared to the most rewarding ones.

➔ What was your biggest accomplishment / failure in this position?

What did you accomplish at work? What were the things you were the proudest of and not really that proud of? During the job interview, your potential employer is going to want to know what you accomplished, and what you didn't, in your current or your previous position.

So how do you answer the interview question about your accomplishments?

You don't want to come across as being arrogant, but you should share your successes on the job. Don't brag about what you've done. Rather, take the time to explain the most important accomplishments at work.

You want to make a connection. The best way to respond to an example of something you accomplished is to directly relate it to the job that you're interviewing for. Review the job posting and the resume. Take the job qualifications and the resume and find the best match. Use it to show the hiring manager that what you accomplished is going to be beneficial to the company you're interviewing with.

When you're asked about the accomplishments, be sure you give some specific examples of what you did in the last position. That example should correlate closely or directly with the job requirements that are listed in the job posting. That way, the interviewer will see that you have the skills necessary to complete the job.

If you wrote a cover letter that was targeted when you applied for the job, then use the information you included to make your reply. For example, if you're interviewing for a position at a school where you'll need to manage student registration, explain to the interviewer how you registered the students for the courses, designed and managed the registration software, and solved the customer's problems.

Let's go over how to answer questions about failures.

If you didn't fail at anything, then you should say so. If you can think of an example, you should be sure it's minor and try to turn it into a positive. For instance, if you're working on a project that's behind deadline, explain to the interviewer how you adjusted your workload and the timeline in order to get back on track and ahead of the schedule again.

Explain and share your solution with them. Explain what caused that failure to happen, and discuss what you did in order to ensure it wouldn't happen again in the future. If you're able to share an example that turned out positive in the end, despite a few hurdles along the way, use that. That way you won't leave your interviewer with the impression that you failed. Instead, you'll show them how you can turn a difficult situation into a positive one.

Try to keep it as positive as you can, but don't blame someone else for what went wrong. Deflecting the blame onto someone else will make a bad impression. Employers don't like to hear that someone else was to blame for your problem.

However, don't make excuses for what happened. Rather, share your solutions for preventing that same failure the following time around. This shows that you're proactive, willing to move forward, and motivated even when things are not going as they were planned.

→ **What were your responsibilities at your current (or last) positions?**

When you are asked questions identified with your present or past positions, it's vital for your reaction to incorporate specifics about what you did in your past position(s). Keep your answer positive — it's a smart thought to raise enhancements or achievements, yet best to avoid saying dissatisfactions or conflicts with associates.

Since this is an exceptionally regular inquiry question, make a point to get ready for it early, and have a decent feeling of how you would condense your obligations regarding each of your positions. By and large, the emphasis will be on your present or latest part.

The most ideal approach is to delineate your obligations from your perspective and to apply them to the employment you are interviewing for. This implies, preceding your meeting that you ought to precisely survey the set of working responsibilities for the new position.

At that point, tie your obligations at your present or past positions in with those of the possible new set of working responsibilities.

By doing this, the business will see that you have the necessary capabilities to carry out the employment.

Concentrate most on your obligations that are specifically identified with the new occupation's necessities. For example, on the off chance that you are meeting for a part that requires administrative aptitudes, underscore ventures you've driven, occasions you've arranged, and individuals you've overseen.

Be unmistakable and take part in your outline of obligations — undoubtedly, the hiring manager has a duplicate of your resume accessible, and is searching for you to go past the data recorded on that report. In any case, abstain from going excessively granular on the subtle elements, such as organization and particular language that can overpower a hiring manager. It can be a troublesome parity, however, attempt to give an intensive depiction of your obligations, and use distinctive dialect from what's on your resume.

Specify a particular case where you profited the organization, tackled an issue, or had a noteworthy achievement. Results-situated answers are useful here. You can say things like "I made a calendar that ceased late conveyance, acquiring the organization's grant for best cooperative person" or "On an everyday premise, I was the essential point of contact with customers, attempting to guarantee that their needs were met, while raising earnest matters."

While you need to outline your obligations in a positive light, it's likewise critical frankly. Try not to adorn your employment title or obligations, since you don't know who the procuring chief will check with when they check your references.

➤ **What were your starting and final levels of compensation?**

Hiring managers expect a possibility for a potential candidate to have the capacity to give the points of interest of their pay history. Be prepared to tell the hiring manager the amount you earned at each of your earlier positions. A business may even ask, "What were your beginning and last levels of pay?"

Questions about pay can be precarious. Ensure your response to this inquiry is straightforward and exact. Likewise, ensure that you disclose to the business any irregularities in your compensation, for example, a pay decrease.

Peruse beneath for tips on the best way to set up an answer, how to reply, and test answers.

The most ideal approach to plan is to survey your pay history. Take note of any adjustments in your compensation throughout every employment, including salary increases, rewards, and different increments in your promotions.

In the event that you are uncertain of the definite measure of your past pay rates, make a point to affirm the right sum. Giving the wrong information to a hiring manager can bring about the hiring manager disavowing the employment offer.

In the event that you experience difficulty recollecting the information, record this data, alongside the dates for every compensation change. You may notwithstanding convey this sheet of paper to the meeting for your reference.

Ensure that what you tell the hiring manager matches what you recorded on your occupation application.

Try not to misrepresent or blow up your income. Numerous businesses will check references and affirm your compensation history before making an occupation offer. An inconsistency between what you reported and what the business says could eliminate you out as a finalist for the employment. Once more, going to the meeting with a pay history recorded can help you keep away from those blunders.

Alongside essentially expressing your beginning and last pay rates, you may likewise list some other advantages you got after some time. These might incorporate rewards or different advantages. Offering these to the hiring manager will exhibit different ways your previous boss perceived your value.

You may likewise take note of any huge changes in obligation that coordinated up with expansions in pay. This will demonstrate that your previous supervisor regarded your work, and remunerated you with new open doors.

At long last, clarify any irregularities in your compensation. For instance, if your compensation diminished for any reason, clarify why. Maybe you changed to low maintenance work while raising a family, or your pay diminished while different types of pay (protection, different advantages, and so forth.) expanded. Demonstrate the point that to the business, you were still an esteemed part, and that your pay appropriately mirrored the work that you did.

"My underlying compensation was $X, and my last pay was $Y. Be that as it may, this doesn't consider the six rewards I got while working there."

"My underlying compensation was $X. Throughout the years, I tackled more obligations, including dealing with my own group and running undertakings; these are the sort of obligations that require a nominal amount of trust and reliance. Because of this increment in obligation, my last pay was $Y."

"When I started working at the organization as a full-time award essayist, my compensation was $X. After some time, that was expanded to $Y, in huge part because of my effective record of accepting stipends. When I transferred to a lesser position of representative, my pay got to be $Z. Be that as it may, I kept on accepting yearly rewards and different incentives for my excellent work."

➤ Who was your best manager and who was the worst?

With the inquiry "Who was your best manager and who was the most noticeably awful?" the hiring manager is attempting to find out if you evaluate fault or convey resentment. The hiring manager, likewise, needs to figure out whether you are a match for the creativity style of the organization.

Regardless of the fact that you had a supervisor who was horrendous, don't say as much. Hiring managers would prefer not to hear an excessive amount of antagonism, and they will ponder what you will say, in regards to their association, on the off chance that you were employed, and it didn't work out.

Take a look at these example interview answers reacting to questions about your best manager.

"I've gained from every manager I've had. From the great ones, what to do, from the testing ones - what not to do. "

"Right off the bat in my vocation, I had a guide who helped me an incredible amount; despite everything, we stay in touch. I've genuinely taken in something from every supervisor I've had. "

"My best supervisor was an administrator who empowered me to tackle more obligations as I advanced in my occupation. I've had different supervisors with a more uninvolved administration style; however, I welcomed the collaboration with the primary manager."

"My best supervisor was a lady who demonstrated to me the significance of positive offerings. She could demonstrate to a client the ideal accessories to pair with an outfit, without being pushy, and taught me to enormously build my proposing capacities."

"I took in a considerable measure of association from my last manager. I've generally been a sorted out individual. However, I adapted better approaches to compose and stimulate the staff from him, which was exceptionally significant for my administration capacities."

"My best supervisor was one who could perceive the qualities in his workers and to use them to their fullest degree. He taught me to take a gander at individuals all the more fully, and understand that practically everybody has something positive to offer."

"My best supervisor was a person who set such a brilliant case for her representatives, that she enlivened individuals to work harder. She was regularly positive, notwithstanding when she wasn't, and never let a client leave despondent. She would dependably have the correct thing to say to give consolation to her clients and representatives alike."

→ **Why are you leaving (did you leave) your job?**

One of the inquiries that are normally asked in an interview is "What is the reason for your leaving your employment?" or "Why did you leave your past occupation?" on the off chance that you have officially proceeded ahead. On the off chance that you were let go from your occupation, utilize these responses to respond.

In the event that you quit voluntarily, take a look at these answers to best determine how to tailor your reaction to meet your specific circumstance. Be direct and focus your interview answer on the future, particularly if you're leaving wasn't under the best of circumstances.

Complete responses to standard prospective employee interview inquiries, similar to this one, ahead of time. Rehearse your reactions so you sound positive, and clear, about your circumstances and your objectives for what's to come.

I became exhausted with the work and found it more difficult. I am a bright worker, and I didn't need my unhappiness to have any effect on the work that I was accomplishing for my manager.

There isn't space for professional development with my present boss, and I'm prepared to proceed onward to another occupation.

I'm searching for a greater job and to develop my profession. It didn't appear to be moral to utilize my previous manager's position.

I was laid-off from my last position when our department was dismantled because of corporate reconstruction.

I'm moving to this region because of family circumstances and left my past position with a specific end goal to make the move.

I've concluded that there are no current positions at my current employer's business for advancement.

Following quite a long while in my last position, I'm searching for an organization where I can contribute and develop in a team environment.

I am keen on another challenge and a chance to utilize my specialized aptitudes and involvement in an alternate position than I did in the past.

I obtained my degree, and I need to use my education in my next position.

I am keen on an occupation with more obligations, and I am very prepared for another challenge.

I left my last position keeping in mind the end goal to invest more energy with my family. Circumstances have changed, and I'm more than prepared for all day employment once more.

I am looking for a position with a steady organization with space for development and open policy for advancement.

I was driving to the city and investing a lot of energy every day on travel. I would like to be nearer to home.

To be completely forthright, I wasn't thinking about a move. In any case, I saw this occupation posting and was charmed by the position and the organization. It sounds like an energizing opportunity and a perfect match with my capabilities.

This position appeared like an incredible match for my abilities and experience, and I am not ready to completely use them in my present employment.

The organization was downsizing and, lamentably, my employment was one of those that were eliminated.

Notwithstanding why you resigned, don't talk severely about your past manager. The hiring manager may think about whether you will be bashing his organization next time you're searching for work.

> **Describe the pace at which you work.**

When you're requested to describe the pace at which you work, be watchful of how you react. This is an inquiry where a quicker response is not necessarily better. Most bosses would rather employ representatives who work at an enduring pace and create quality results. Somebody who is too laid back to take care of business, in a sensible time period, won't be a decent employee, nor is an applicant who works excitedly throughout the day because they may make more mistakes, or ultimately wear out.

One approach to answering this question is to say that you work at an enduring pace; however you normally finish work ahead of time. You additionally need to underline that you accomplish quality results at your pace. Give a particular case of a period when working at this pace helped you accomplish results.

Examine your capacity to oversee deadlines and complete them on, or ahead, of time. In the event that you work at a vocation where you have set criteria (i.e. number of calls made or responded to) that measures achievements, talk about how you have accomplished or surpassed those objectives.

I for the most part work at a relentless, reliable pace. In light of my capacity to sort out and arrange my work routine, I generally finish my work early. For instance, when I was given a huge task due in six months, I broke the undertaking into expansive objectives and little, everyday objectives. I made a calendar, and consistently scratched off each of these objectives, while still effectively finishing my different obligations. I eventually completed the undertaking a week ahead of schedule.

I see myself as an industrious laborer who keeps away from uncertainty. At my past employment, we needed to make no less than 30 calls each month, on top of our other regulatory obligations. While some individuals put off all their obligations to the end of their work day, which some of the time prompted individuals to miss their responsibilities, I separated my time between making calls and doing my different requirements. I am not easily sidetracked, but rather can adjust working relentlessly on various undertakings. This permits me to finish the majority of my work on time and deliver quality results. I won best sales representative three times at my past organization.

➙ How do you view yourself? Who do you compare yourself to?

Keeping in mind the end goal to evaluate your qualities and shortcomings during an interview, a business may request that you describe yourself. This sort of inquiry can take different structures, from "How would you see yourself?" to "Whom would you compare yourself with?" An inquiry like this likewise permits bosses to perceive how you see yourself.

The most ideal approach to answering is to share some of your qualities, especially those that match the capabilities for the occupation.

Notwithstanding examining qualities that are integral to the employment, you may likewise incorporate some other fascinating individual qualities that are identified with the position, yet will give a legitimate feel to your presentation. You can then quickly clarify how that quality associates with your vocation.

For instance, for a position in publicizing, you may specify how you see yourself as an imaginative kind of individual and after that, likewise, say that you are a daring person who appreciates skydiving or bungee jumping.

You can then include that you bring some of that risk taking into group environments and are unafraid of attempting new, imaginative ideas to reach new levels of progress.

Be prepared for subsequent inquiries, for example, a solicitation for you to refer to situations of whatever qualities that you say. Be prepared to reference circumstances where you connected that quality and the effect which you had. For instance, on the off chance that you say you are an imaginative individual, you can specify a specific venture in which you thought outside the box and how that endeavor helped you obtain another customer.

A different line of subsequent questioning may be to inquire as to whether you have supplied an absolutely positive viewpoint of yourself. The most ideal approach to an answer is to say a shortcoming that won't specifically ruin the outcome of the interview. For instance, communicate one that is not vital to the occupation, could be understood as a quality, or one that you've dealt with to the point that it is not really a shortcoming. For instance, you may say that you have taken a shot at your oral presentation aptitudes persistently in the course of recent years with the goal that you can now give certain, lucid, and outwardly captivating presentations to customers.

A few managers may request that you compare yourself with another person keeping in mind the end goal to decide all the more unmistakably how you see yourself. By and large, you ought to take an unobtrusive approach and abstain from comparing yourself with notorious figures in business, legislative issues or the comedy world.

A superior respect can be to say a specifically motivating individual, for example, a more established kin, guardian, educator or guide. The key will be to call attention to some positive, normal quality that makes you comparable, and that matches the occupation capabilities. For instance, you may say "I'm a lot like my Dad; he is a craftsman who ingrained in me my feeling of inventiveness and my enthusiasm for imaginative risk taking."

In noting this question, the key is to arrive at an answer that presents you in a positive light, yet is, in the meantime, unassuming and genuine.

➤ **If you could relive the last 10 years of your life, what would you do differently?**

At the point when asking what you would do on the off chance that you could relive your life, the hiring manager is searching for an imperfection in your interview. Never forget, the objective for the initial few meetings is to get the following interview. For the hiring manager, it is to weed out whatever number of candidates as would be prudent. Here's where an individual answer could work.

I lost my mom to Alzheimer's. I wish I'd understood more about the disease to support me through that troublesome time.

Truly, nothing. I've gained from every experience I've had.

I am entirely fulfilled by the vocation I've picked and how it has advanced. I have learned critical things at each stage and from the customers I have worked with.

I have had individuals ask me in the past if I would have been more satisfied if I had begun in my present occupation as opposed to starting in the corporate world. I am exceptionally happy that I have my involvement in business, as I think it gives me one of a kind understanding and point of view that I generally wouldn't have.

Despite the fact that I cherish what I do now, I wouldn't change how I got here.

↣ **What are you passionate about?**

When you're gotten some information about a prospective employee interview, it's a decent chance to share diversions, enthusiasms, or whatever is important in your life.

Businesses pose this question to take in more about your own advantages and values, furthermore to understand irrespective of whether you are a committed individual.

Hiring managers are also hoping to see that you're a balanced individual, with an existence outside of the workplace. Your response to this inquiry can uncover whether you will be a solid match with the organization society. While nevertheless you need to be cautious and insightful by the way you react, attempt to be real in your reaction, and show how you connect with your interests.

Your reaction doesn't have to be centered on work; however, it ought to show your capacity to give yourself to a specific activity or side interest about which you are enthusiastic.

Whatever your reaction, give a few cases of how you have devoted yourself to that intrigue or movement.

You can likewise say objectives, (for example, preparing for a race, if running is your obsession), which gives hiring managers a feeling of your long haul intuition and steadiness.

The hiring manager may get some information about your drive, so ensure it's something you feel good talking about. On the off chance that film is your obsession, for instance, hiring managers may request motion picture proposals, or ask about your most loved motion picture.

Regardless of what you answer is, make certain that what you share isn't something that could possibly cut into your working hours. For instance, you would prefer not to say that you're a mountain climber with the objective of climbing Mount Everest soon or that you're getting prepared for the Tour de France or hoping to spend the winters skiing in Aspen.

One of my most noteworthy interests is helping other people. When I was more youthful, I delighted in helping my mother with family home repairs. As I developed responsibility, that tendency grew, and I sought to help other people too. I like filling needs that meet their particular requirements.

I'm energetic about painting. I take a night art class once per week and attempt to find time every weekend to paint. Painting is a decent path for me to unwind following a busy week.

I lost my dad to pancreatic disease and since that time, I have invested energy volunteering in bringing issues to light and funding for tumor research. I volunteer for PanCan, a support group, and I'm a member of their volunteer system. Something I'm energetic about is helping with finding a cure, however I can. I additionally love becoming more acquainted with patients and survivors on an individual level.

I'm energetic about having any kind of effect. When I'm designated a task at work, I need to do my best to make progress. I feel the same way about what I do in my own life.

I'm enthusiastic about preparing: I cherish the procedure of looking into new formulas and testing them out.

➤ **What are your pet peeves?**

A business may pose the question "What are your pet peeves?" for a couple reasons. Your answer will help the interviewer out whether you would be a solid match inside the organization's society. For instance, on the off chance that you say you are irritated by group ventures, and the employment includes a considerable measure of coordinated effort, this may not be the position for you. Your answer will likewise demonstrate to the business how easily annoyed you are. On the off chance that your answer is a long tirade of lots of things that truly irritate you, you may give off an impression of being a disagreeable individual to work with.

This inquiry may appear to be troublesome, on the grounds that it gets some information about things that bother you, which could lead you to sound negative or obnoxious. In any case, when addressed consciously, this inquiry can show why you are a solid contender for the position.

There are a couple approaches to effectively answer this inquiry. Regardless of how you reply, abstain from sounding negative. Whatever particular annoyance you say, make light of the amount it troubles you.

Abstain from utilizing very spirited dialect that will make you appear to be irritated or offensive. Talk placidly, and make it clear that whatever it is that disturbs you doesn't keep you from doing your own particular work or getting on with your day.

Some individuals like to reply by saying they have no pet peeves by any means. In any case, this answer may seem to be untrustworthy, in light of the fact that everybody is troubled by something. A superior answer will concentrate on something that does not trouble you in particular, that can control, and that does not make you look bad as a worker.

One approach to answering this inquiry is to concentrate on a particular vexation that is disconnected to the employment (for instance, your pet peeve may be individuals who don't utilize their turn signals when they drive). This sort of answer will keep you from saying something negative that is identified with the employment.

You can likewise portray a pet peeve that is identified with the work environment, and that would really be a negative for the occupation. For instance, if the occupation includes a great deal of collaboration, you may say your outstanding irritation is the point at which a man can't adequately work with a group. Nonetheless, make certain to then clarify how you would manage that circumstance.

You may likewise turn this inquiry around and underline your own particular exertion measurements. For instance, you may say that you dislike when individuals don't push themselves to go past the absolute minimum, so you are continually pushing yourself to accomplish the best results on any venture.

In the event that you asked my teenage girl, she would most likely let you know my pet peeve is the volume of her music and the mess in her room. In any case, I don't have any other pet peeves. On the off chance that something is bothering me, I venture back, break down "why," and arrive at a logical solution.

I don't care for when individuals have negative states of mind, especially in the working environment. I jump at the chance to stay constructive, notwithstanding amid a troublesome circumstance, and don't give individuals' negative mentalities a chance to influence me.

I dislike when I see a colleague declining to take care of his or her fair share on an undertaking. As colleagues, we must help the entire group make progress. When I see somebody not doing his or her assignment, I communicate clearly and positively with the group about my worries, and attempt to think of an answer, for example, redistributing a portion of the responsibilities.

One particular pet peeve is when individuals are frequently late. My child is continually running late for school, so I have been attempting to impart punctuality in him. Convenience is likewise critical in the working environment.

⇥ What can we expect from you in the first 60 days on the job?

So as to make sense of how you will approach another job, a hiring manager may make an inquiry like, "What would we be able to anticipate from you in the initial 60 days at work?"

This is an extreme inquiry, as there are numerous approaches to answer it. Most managers will search for workers who will be as independent as could be expected under the circumstances amid their preparation period and who will endeavor to make critical commitments from the get-go.

You ought to demonstrate that you'll take a self-assured way to deal with completing your job without annoying your supervisor, and point out that you'll make it a priority to be gainful inside your initial few days at work.

I will contact every one of the partners in my specialty and interview divisions to learn as much as could reasonably be expected about the roles that different people play inside the business. I will learn all the information which you have referenced on the occupation.

At night, I'll keep perusing all that I can discover about the organization and industry to get an exact fix on the condition of the firm inside the commercial sector. Our expert affiliation offers some online instructional exercises on cutting edge Excel macros so I will chip away at those amid my off hours.

This kind of inquiry additionally gives an opening to you to avow your capacity to learn rapidly and add esteem in key zones of the work at an early stage in your position. In view of the expected set of responsibilities, alongside anything your hiring manager has said in regards to the position's principle obligations, present a strategy for how your skill set will prepare you to take on those key obligations quickly.

For instance, you may say "You have emphasized the significance of composing convincing public statements, and taking into account my involvement in the senator's office, I surmise that I will have the capacity to jump in and tackle that obligation at an early stage."

You can likewise affirm that you'll take orders from your supervisor and center your energies on acing the main components of your work amid the initial few weeks so you can do well at the earliest opportunity.

Furthermore, managers tend to support objective, organized, and all around composed representatives. Along these lines, you ought to share some understanding about your procedure for tackling a responsibility, such as taking on another obligation. You may reference your inclination for setting daily and weekly learning objectives.

Remember that incessant intrusions by new staff can baffle managers. You could include that you will arrange a rundown of inquiries that couldn't be replied to through e-mail as you experience your day-by-day schedule. At that point, say that you would deliver these inquiries to your chief or her designee at setting up times to shield your manager from less than ideal intrusions.

➤ What is the worst thing that you have gotten away with?

"What is the most noticeably bad thing that you have gotten away with?" This is an uncommon inquiry question; yet a few managers request this information in order to gain insight into of your personality and behavior, and whether you would fit in with the organization. A business may ask this as an approach to ensure you have not done anything that may be viewed as a caution for the position.

This is one of those precarious explorative questions. You should not say that you never did anything that you have gotten away with, on the grounds that no one is perfect. Then again, you certainly don't need your "most exceedingly bad thing" to be something truly terrible, for example, something unlawful, dishonest, or coldblooded.

One approach to an answer is to keep it on the light side. For instance, you may give a case of something minor that you escaped with that includes your folks or school (staying out late, pulling a trick, and so forth.).

You may likewise turn the inquiry around and rather give a case of the "best" thing you got away with.

For instance, you may clarify that you helped a companion, and he or she never discovered it was you. In any case, you would prefer not to sound immaculate so you may finish up with a speedy, carefree case of something naughtier that you escaped with.

The thing to recall with the suspicious inquiries is that it's fine to pause for a minute or two to outline a reaction. At that point, be straightforward, generally, so you are addressing the inquiry, however not in a way that would make the hiring manager not have any desire to hire you. Keep it positive as much as you can.

There isn't a correct response to these sorts of inquiries. Or maybe, the interviewer will consider how your react.

I've never been a lot of a troublemaker, even as a young person. I assume the greatest thing I ever escaped with was a school trick I sorted out and orchestrated. We flipped around the majority of the work areas in each classroom. I wanted to have a fabulous time, positive associations with my friends, in spite of the fact that I think my tricking days are over!

While this is really a positive thing, the greatest thing I escaped with was helping arrange a surprise get-away for an exhausted friend. We arranged the entire thing without her discovering until we took her to the airplane terminal! Obviously, I've escaped with a couple less positive things as well – I'm certain I stayed out past bedtime a couple times without my folks finding out!

⇥ What philosophy guides your work?

Hiring managers for expert positions in ranges like directing, nursing, educating and administration will frequently ask about the methodology that you take to your work. They may pose these questions to get a feeling of your qualities or to figure out whether your theory is predictable with their business model.

The hiring manager may likewise be trying to check whether you have stayed aware of trends in your field. In any case, the business will look for an unmistakable, sound explanation, so they realize what's in store for you as a representative.

To set up your answer, begin by looking into the mission statement of the organization you're interviewing with. The mission statement ought to be accessible on the organization's site.

In the event that you have any professional associations at the organization, you can likewise set up an instructive interview to find out about the working environment.

It might do to take a look at a portion of the scholars who have formed current practices in your field; however, it is recommended that you specify that you are diverse in your approach, customizing your activities while taking into account the circumstance.

Simply ensure you can portray the particular approaches you regularly take to arrive at your answer.

At the point when asking follow-up inquiries, hiring managers may request cases of how you have used your knowledge. Along these lines, be prepared to depict particular circumstances, moves you made, and the positive results you produced through your methodology.

⇥ What type of work environment do you prefer?

At the point when you're getting ready for an interview, it's a smart thought to consider how you will answer questions about what sort of workplace you incline toward. The hiring manager will attempt to set up how well you will fit in at the organization, with the organization society, and in what environment you are generally useful.

The most ideal approach to get ready for inquiries like this is to ensure you do your research. Organization sites contain a lot of data about the organization environment, expressed and inferred. There are normally tabs that are labeled, "About Us," which highlight the hard-working attitude of the organization overall, and some of the time, give data on individual representatives.

On the off chance that you have a contact at the organization, talk with them about the organization culture. Connect with your friend to discover information in regards to the reputation of the organization you are applying to. In all actuality, it will be exceptionally useful to you to dissect what the workplace will be, on the grounds that it will influence how happy and useful you will be in the event that you land the position.

Here and there, it's unrealistic to get some answers concerning the workplace at a specific organization. All things considered, it's fine to get some information about the organization culture, and plan your answer in anticipation of what they say. When you know how they see their workplace, you can figure out whether you'll be a solid match, and can offer examples of how your work style coordinates well with their way of life.

When you have obtained some information about the environment, your most solid option is to attempt to stay generally neutral, since, at this phase in the interview procedure, you don't know actually what it will be like working for the organization. It's a smart thought to assert that you are adaptable and adjust cheerfully in any environment. You wouldn't have any desire to say anything to harm your odds of getting to the following stage in the recruiting process.

I can be adaptable with regards to my workplace. From your site, it would appear that the environment in the Engineering division here at RRS, Inc. is quick paced and organized to encompass peers. I appreciate working in a zone that is fast paced, and I imagine that on multiple occasions, this sort of environment is helpful for new thoughts and applications.

I have worked in numerous sorts of workplaces and delighted in taking in new things from each. I would say that while I don't have an inclination for a specific situation, I truly like working with individuals who are focused on completing things and who are energetic about their work.

As a rule, I get a kick out of the chance to work in a domain where efficiency is high, and the representatives have a feeling of duty. As far as I can tell, whether the way of life is to a great degree quick paced, or more laid back, it's the devotion of the representatives at all levels that makes the organization effective and an awesome work environment.

I appreciate working in a domain where the individuals from the group have a solid feeling of comradery and a decent hard-working attitude. I like working with able, kind, interesting individuals who like to complete things. It's essential to me to feel that I can trust my colleagues to dependably put forth a valiant effort since I do.

Having worked in an assortment of workplaces, from extremely easygoing and laid back to super quick-paced, I think I adjust well to most. I'm not acquainted with what the professional workplace is here, would you be able to tell me about it?

➤ When do you plan on retiring?

Despite the fact that it appears to be uncalled for, bosses can be worried about to what extent a more established applicant will stay on the off chance that they are enlisted. They can be reluctant to put the time and cash in procuring and preparing a worker who may resign in a year or two.

Asking a candidate an inquiry question about when they plan to resign is an approach to test the job responsibility of a more seasoned specialist.

Your response to this inquiry ought to obviously suffice, as you are truly committed to your profession and not simply investing your effort until retirement.

A decent answer can express that you aren't thinking about retirement soon since you are so enthusiastic about the work you are doing in your field.

Notice particular ventures and obligations in your present or last position which are empowering and compensating. Make certain to specify the parts of the occupation for which you are interviewing that speak to you and would inspire you to put the most effort in your work.

Another approach to get the message across that you're not prepared for retirement is to examine your objectives for expert improvement.

Managers may scrutinize the vitality level of the more seasoned worker, so give examples of how you may have gone the additional mile in late activities to meet a due date or awe a customer. On the off chance that you frequently work more than the base hours in your occupation, figure out how to coordinate your work routine into the interview. For instance, maybe you get a kick out of the chance to get to work right on time to compose your day and/or stay later to get ready for the following day.

➤ Would you rather be liked or respected?

Hiring managers will utilize a wide range of inquiries to figure out what kind of worker you would be if employed.

Questions like, "Would you rather be respected or liked?" can furnish the hiring manager with an understanding into what persuades you as you communicate with colleagues and clients.

Despite the fact that there is no right response to this inquiry, and your accentuation may fluctuate in light of the setting of your employment, here are some broad rules to consider while noting this sort of inquiry.

In most workplaces, being regarded ought to be given more noteworthy attention, since it is normally connected to capability and success. Be that as it may, a huge variable to consider is the way of you associate with your partners.

For instance, on the off chance that you are vying for an administrative or official part, you ought to positively stress that being regarded would be a need for you so that your workers will eagerly complete your orders.

It is imperative to include that, in spite of the fact that getting regard from subordinates is important to a supervisory part, so too is giving admiration. Ensure that you express that you comprehend the corresponding way of expert and individual connections.

In parts where cooperation and collegiality are essential, you can reference your enthusiasm for being well liked, keeping in mind the end goal to make a symphonious work group.

In the event that you are interviewing for a position that includes successive contact with customers, in which a charming nature is required to set up affinity or keep up a positive relationship, then you ought to say the advantage of being liked concerning this segment of you work.

You will likewise need to convey information and duties; so respect will likewise be critical with a specific end goal to create trust in your clients.

Most hiring managers will acknowledge a nuanced answer in which you specify the estimation of both being respected and liked. In any case, you ought to be set up to examine the relative significance of either if pressed.

The most basic part of your reaction will be the reason you provide your answers and how you associate your statements to viably doing some portion of your share.

For instance, you may say, "At work, I would rather be respected. My success as a salesman has stemmed to a great extent from my capacity to foresee the necessities and issues of my clients and to show my products as an approach to address and take care of those issues. When admiration has been built up, I find that my clients keep coming back to me for extra direction. Obviously, I need my customers to like me too, and I do the seemingly insignificant details, like presenting to them to a favorite lunch or taking them for a round of golf so that they, likewise, see the individual value of our relationship."

Similarly as with most inquiries, you ought to be set up for a subsequent inquiry requesting clarification or an example of how you have shown in the past whatever you are stating. In the case above, you may be asked "Would you be able to give me a case of how you picked up the admiration of a client previously?" as a subsequent inquiry. Accordingly, you could say:

One of my new customers was worried about the amount of important material that was utilized as a part of the manufacturing process. I conveyed her to a plant where our gear was being used and showed how productively it used assets. I helped her price out the payback plan in the event that she bought the new machine, and she could compose a support that was endorsed by her supervisor. She has called upon me for guidance frequently from that point forward and kept on acquiring our products.

⤳ Why are you interested in a lower level job?

It is not extraordinary for laborers, who are more seasoned, unemployed, over focused on, adjusting family duties or basically tired of working too hard, to look for a lower level position.

The employing director will ask you for what reason you are keen on a lower level occupation than you're qualified for.

You will normally be asked to clarify for what valid reason you will surrender status, pay and obligation. The best approach will be to outline your answer emphatically with an emphasis on the appealing components of your objective employment. Along these lines, you will clarify why you are moving towards the lower level occupation rather than far from your higher paying position.

Make a list of the responsibilities connected with your prospective position, which is generally engaging. Consider examples of when you have completed comparative errands and connected comparative abilities before.

Be prepared to reference the achievements you accomplished in those circumstances and the level of fulfillment that you gained.

Search for any association between the alluring parts of your present place of employment and the potential position. For instance, as a building manager, the most empowering part of your present work may be to investigate plan issues going up against your group of designers. This reference would bolster your goal to get back on the forefronts doing designing revisions instead of administration assignments.

Another conceivable advantage could be to say any reduced requirements for money amid the present period of your life, especially in the event that you initially tackled the most elevated amount of work basically for financial purposes. For instance, possibly you have youngsters who have now graduated school or have scaled back your home.

Then again, in case you're applying for an hourly employment versus a salaried or administration position, you could say that you were working a lot of hours every week, and you're currently searching for fewer obligations and a fairly lighter workload.

The key will be to match these statements with one in regards to your enthusiasm for the kind of occupation you're applying for.

➤ Why are you interested in a non-management job?

Reacting to questions about your desire to downshift from an administrative occupation to a master position can be exceptionally dubious. Possibly you are a business manager who now needs to retreat to deals, a manager who needs to be an author once more, or an administrator who needs to get again into the classroom. Your challenge in representing your longing to downshift is to answer the inquiry without appearing like you need inspiration or are searching for a simpler position.

One method is to outline your answer as an individual inclination for the new position, while stressing your prosperity and fulfillment in the more elevated position. It will benefit particular examples of how you were compelling as a director and how you affected all that really matters.

Start by specifying parts of your management position which you delighted in, and paint a general picture of no less than a modest level fulfillment. Abstain from griping about the difficulties and challenges of overseeing others, since your hiring manager may start to view you as somebody who has issues interacting with associates or who abstains from assuming responsibility.

Next, it's critical to disclose what pulls you to the non-administration position you're looking for. Make a point to be specific. In the event that possible talk about the achievement you may have had in the non-administration employments you had before. Tell stories concerning your achievements in the position, and portray your level of fulfillment with eagerness. Much of the time, you will go back to an earlier position; for instance, you may examine your experience an architect before turning into a designing executive.

Ensure that you likewise fuse any case of how you performed an expert part as a major aspect of your administration obligations and how that felt for you. For instance, a business supervisor may mediate to bring a big deal to a close with a noteworthy client occasionally. That kind of experience can be the ideal story point for disclosing your motivation to come back to the earlier position.

Finally, you will need your hiring manager to understand that you are seeking the new position on merits and not as an approach to get away from an unacceptable or troublesome part as a manager.

➤ Why should I take a risk on you?

Numerous businesses are worried about creating an arrival on their speculation with new employees; so they hope to hire individuals who think they will make an enduring addition to the organization. In case you're changing professions, for example, you may be asked, "Why would it be a good idea for me to take a risk on you since you've changed fields fairly recently?"

In your answer, you'll have to address any worries the business may have about to what extent you will stay in the employment. This is particularly vital if your resume shows that you've had different new positions inside a brief time frame.

The most ideal approach to answering this sort of inquiry is to stress how well this specific position fits your interests. Audit every component of the expected set of responsibilities and note the obligations that are most fascinating to you. Consider similar positions you've had in the past and be prepared to portray how satisfying that position was for you.

Position yourself as a solution, not a potential danger. Match what you bring to the table to the rundown of employment prerequisites, and give your best attempt to close the deal, accentuating the qualities and attributes that make you a special and strong match for the occupation.

From our discussion, it appears as though you're searching for somebody to come in and assume the responsibility for your publication division. With my seven years of experience working in online and print distribution, I have spared organizations a large number of dollars by working effectively with consultants. In my last occupation, I hit the ground running, managing fifty off-webpage editors and surveyed issues rapidly with our web design team. I'm ready to stay centered in upsetting circumstances, for example, when we expanded our article creation by fifty percent month over month.

Research your new profession field altogether and present a definite clarification concerning why you are rolling out the improvement. Talk with contacts working in your new field and shadow them to pick up a more top-to-bottom perspective of their position. In the event that you can, understudy or volunteer for a brief span to demonstrate to potential bosses that you are educated about the field and focused on your new part.

On the off chance that you think your job history may bring a warning up, with respect to your level of responsibility to every employment you've held, stress how your past experience has driven you to this field and the courses in which has reinforced your certainty for this new position.

For instance, you may specify that before, you changed fields on account of the charm of a higher compensation, more obligation or more prominent status, yet didn't precisely consider how rigorous the real function would be. You can specify that you developed from that experience and are prepared to completely focus on another position.

Conclusion

Thank you again for downloading this book!

I hope this book was able to help you to understand how to excel in your next interview by answering all the questions in a way that impresses your potential employer.

The next step is to implement what you have learned. Finally, if you enjoyed this book, would you be kind enough to leave a review for this book on Amazon?

Thank you and good luck!

www.ingramcontent.com/pod-product-compliance
Lightning Source LLC
Chambersburg PA
CBHW060402190526
45169CB00002B/714